AMERICA IS AN IDEA
AND THE AMERICAN DREAM
IS FOR EVERYONE

Why We Built empowr.com:
The Experiment to Democratize Social Media

Michael Cyrus Pousti

ISBN: 978-0-69251-039-1

Published by empowr, San Diego, California

To my amazing mom...
For a lifetime of unconditional love and support, giving and self-sacrifice

To my incredible dad...
For leadership by example and the gifts of focus and swimming

And to my beautiful Jasmin, Sydney, and Sky...
For unwavering love, forgiveness and ensuring I never take myself too seriously

TABLE OF CONTENTS

A QUICK INTRODUCTION

It was a cold, rainy Monday in San Diego. Southern California doesn't much like the rain *or* the cold, and the seemingly dark mood of the city perfectly matched my own gloomy state. I sat in my apartment and looked down at the inked page in my hands. Everything seemed a bit surreal, but it finally dawned on me: *it was all over now*. The entire business, my plans for its future, the people whose lives it was supposed to improve, the sweeping changes it was supposed to bring to a broken system—all of them had slipped through my fingers like fine grains of sand.

I thought back to the day, in April 2000, when our army of investment banks and financial institutions, attorneys and accountants filed with the United States Securities and Exchange Commission to take our company public on the stock exchange (IPO). We had celebrated with bottles of Dom Pérignon and toasted the important milestone. That was only six months ago, but it felt like it had been decades ago. Things had gone downhill *very* quickly. After countless flights to every corner of the country to meet with investors whom I thought I could convince to save us, endless hours of advice from friends, attorneys and accountants, and all my other efforts, ultimately I had failed.

It was October 2000, and the dot-com bubble had burst, quickly turning *my* thriving dot-com into a dot-bomb. Just a few days after we filed to get public, the U.S. tech-heavy NASDAQ stock market began its long and sharp dive. Investors were not yet educated enough to separate the good tech companies from the bad, so every business with a dot-com in its name was being dropped overnight like a bad habit. The opportunity to go public was completely shut down for all companies; we missed the window for becoming a public traded company and instantly raising hundreds of millions of dollars in an initial public offering (IPO) by just a few weeks; even industry-leading giants like Yahoo that had already gone public would see their stock prices plummet by over 90%.

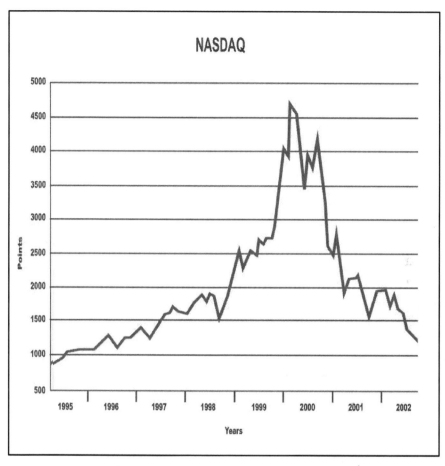

Drop in NASDQAQ starting in April 2000[1]

Although it had been a long, hard-fought battle, outside economic pressures that were beyond anyone's control had proven to be foes too strong for me to defeat. In the end, my Internet portal for college students, CollegeClub.com—the world's leading website for 18-24 year olds and the business I'd personally invested millions of dollars and seven years of my life in—had finally been chopped up into pieces and sold off. And, despite all my best efforts, this sale of my company pulled the rug out from under me and my 4,000 employees who, in an earlier red-hot economy, had chosen to forgo other opportunities and pursue my mission.

I thought back to the day thirteen years before when, as a senior undergraduate student, I had made the decision to stand up and march out of my classes—forever. I'd decided that enough was enough. Not only would I not finish my computer science degree, which I had spent almost four years pursuing, but instead I thought I would start a company and change the entire educational system—using software—so no one else would have to endure the expensive mess that was called "higher education," at least not in the way I had experienced it for my entire adult life.

I thought back to how I had started my first company on the day after dropping out of university. My sole focus had been to generate the millions of dollars that I figured I'd need to build my visionary university-disrupting entity.

I thought about how hard I had worked to make my first company succeed, only to be required, as a bright-eyed and bushy-tailed twenty-one-year-old, to defy all odds and go up against the federal government, in its own courtrooms, to prove that the exponential "hockey stick" growth and success that I was experiencing were legitimate and deserved.

And I thought back to my next move (in 1993, after the courts ordered the government to release my millions of dollars that it had been holding) to finally start CollegeClub.com with dreams of providing a truly accountable educational system that would deliver to students a real education and four of the best years of their lives, in exchange for their time and money...

I had not stopped running for thirteen years, and I was tired and beat up. Mentally, physically, and financially exhausted.

And yet, in that state of mind, I had no idea that the thirteen-year struggle behind me would pale in comparison to the following fourteen years.

Everything is relative, and, looking back, I didn't *really* understand the meaning of physical and mental exhaustion.

Indeed, it would be fair for you to think that, after all this, I would say *"SCREW IT!"* and give up on the higher purpose that I was pursuing. That I would instead, find a way to recoup my financial losses and try to make a living. Indeed, a different (possibly smarter or saner) person might have. But, thanks in large part to my stubborn nature, I couldn't just give up on my goals. I felt that I had lost a battle but not the war. And, despite my near complete exhaustion, I was still eager to get back in the fight.

I knew that, even though I was tired and defeated, the months of negotiations, stress, and fighting had given me a certain mental toughness that I might lose if I took a break. I was eager to apply that toughness and get back in the game. So eager, in fact, that on a Thursday—only three days after CollegeClub.com was sold off—I documented a new strategy for not just rebuilding totally from scratch but for leapfrogging my college approach and building an entire economic ecosystem (which I will describe in this book) that, of course, would also include *the educational system I envisioned.*

The journey that I've been on since that Thursday, way back in the year 2000, has included years of trial and error, inspiring inventions, shattering losses, and debilitating stress-related health problems. The team that I've formed over the years to help make my vision a reality has sacrificed and endured right along with me. Together we've walked away from untold millions of dollars in financial offers, because we all decided that, at some point in the future, accepting those investments *might* conflict with our goals. We didn't want to compromise on our mission or risk having to start over. Our staying away from the sometimes moody, often corrupt financial system has meant that we have had a better chance to stay focused on our work, even when it has meant eating ramen noodles or living on friends' and family's sofas for a few years.

One of the interesting (if seemingly obvious) things about walking away from piles of money offered to us, in order to pursue a life of purpose is that it has a surprisingly negative effect on your net worth.

All joking aside, I'm not telling you this story in some macho attempt to impress you or to gain your sympathy. I'm trying to convey how passionately devoted my team and I have been to accomplishing a very specific goal.

This book is dedicated to explaining that goal in a way that (I hope) is easy for readers to understand. Some of this book will attempt to explain our take on history and some of the scary directions we're afraid the world is headed. We'll discuss what my team and I are trying to do about it—***with empowr.com***—and some of the strategies and approaches we're taking as we work toward our goal. But before we jump neck-deep into the meat of the book, I think I should first get something out of the way.

MY CONFESSION

I'm neither a professional writer nor an expert in all of the fields that I discuss in this book, but I am a pretty good computer scientist who is just pigheaded enough to believe that he can make the world a better place for millions of people if he works hard enough, keeps getting back up every time he gets knocked down, and surrounds himself with the right team.

Before we go any further into what has motivated and driven me and my team so hard and for so long, I want to make a small confession. I'm not a professional writer, so I recognize that this book may have shortcomings. I'm not a political scientist or economist, either, and don't pretend to be an expert in many of the fields that I write about in these pages. I have great respect for those people who have a deeper knowledge than I of those areas. To achieve my goals, however, I don't need to be an expert.

One of the goals of this book is to encourage a lively discussion around the problems that I present and my proposed solutions. I sincerely hope that experts, intellectuals, and specialists in each of the referenced fields will become part of that discussion.

Now that I've been candid about who I am *not*, I do want to tell you about who and what I *am*.

I am a computer scientist that was fortunate to discover at a very early age that he had a talent (software development) and who was inspired by a handful of economists, a few self-help gurus, and some psychology theories. Those men injected big ideas into my head about my own capabilities and motivated me to pursue a life of purpose (or "self-actualization," as Abraham Maslow calls it) without self-limiting beliefs. And they did that with impeccable timing: precisely at a time when I was experiencing monetary success and realizing how empty that felt because it wasn't accompanied by a strong sense of purpose.

It's worth noting that I was also lucky enough to be born into a family that, starting with my grandmother, has given away the majority of its wealth to charitable causes, primarily for the building and operating of orphanages that have enabled thousands of children to receive a respectable room and board and a solid education all the way up to and including a higher education. And they did it quietly and without the usual chest-beating, look-at-me, and stick-my-name-on-everything fanfare that we've somewhat grown to expect from philanthropists. If you ever meet my parents or had met my grandmother before she passed, you'd have a hard time believing the level of their contributions because of how much humility they possess and how simply they live their lives.

When you have that type of real-life example to look up to in your home, and then further hit the jackpot when you discover your talent at a young age, you can't help but feel like you simply don't have the right to live your life in the service of yourself.

It turns out that pursuing a life of purpose can be a hell of a lot more difficult than it sounds. But, in setting and pursuing that goal over the years, I've created a number of businesses designed to make the world better in the hopes of finding the personal and professional fulfillment that I have been chasing. That said, I'm not so delusional as to believe that anything my team and I come up with will change the world overnight or that any of them will be wonder drugs that cure the world's ailments.

Always faced with the next big challenge or obstacle, my team and I live in constant fear that not only won't we ultimately succeed, but that we may not even make it to the next chapter of our evolution. So, with this book, I also hope to inspire others to pick up the ball if we drop it. We'll gladly share our experiences, strategies, and even patented technologies.

I know that a bunch of people and companies claim to be open to sharing their patents and technology; behind closed doors, though, they make sure their lawyers keep everything locked up tight. I take pride not just in talking the talk but also in walking the walk when it comes to this aspect of what we do. For proof of this, please feel free to look at all of the companies that use our patented technologies but against which we are not pursuing any form of legal action, including Facebook, Twitter, and virtually all social media platforms in existence today. *If they offer third-party application developers the ability to launch apps in their platforms; or utilize transactions, a credit system, virtual currency, conduct transactions over mobile devices* (or any of a few dozen other critical technologies that are essential to their revenue models and existence), *they are using technologies that we invented and patented.*

To review our patents for yourself, simply visit www.Google.com/Patents and enter my last name (Pousti) into the search field.

The primary reason for our strategy is not generosity or altruism; rather, it's selfishness. We freely share our intellectual property because we believe, in doing so, our own personal and professional goals will be achieved more quickly and thoroughly. And for us, achieving those goals is more important than the money and prestige that could come from monopolizing our patents and technology.

Thank you for purchasing this book and taking the time to read it. I've purposely written it in a concise format. Most of the people interested in reading a book like this are consumed by their own projects; reading a long book is a luxury they can't always afford. So I've edited each section down to bite-size. Even the busiest person should be able to find time to flip through it. I have also encapsulated my key concepts in the titles and topic paragraphs of each section.

I very much hope that you get a lot out of the reading experience and that, by the end, you will share at least a small part of my passion for what the empowr team and I are trying to accomplish. Perhaps you'll even gain some inspiration and launch your own start-up, which would delight me and my team. So, with these caveats behind me, I'll give you the quick and dirty on what you're going to read about.

WHAT THIS BOOK IS ALL ABOUT

Two of the most important things that contributed to the success of First World countries (democracy and education) have eroded over the years, with dire consequences. My team and I have a few ideas about how to fix these broken systems—using technology. I write about it on the following pages.

Even if you disagree with us and believe the system is working as it should and that our world is heading in the right direction, I hope to convince you that improving and expanding these pillars of civilization is still a worthy endeavor.

This book is about why and how my team and I are creating a business that we hope will do its part to help foster a new online culture, one that uses some of the most powerful wealth-creating forces in our world (democracy, education, and network technology) to help fight the biggest global problems we face (poverty and inequality; extremism and terrorism; and instability of every kind through the unraveling of democracy in numerous countries).

So that you know where I'm coming from, I will begin by telling you briefly why I think democracy, western education, and network technology have "saved the world"; and how each of them is now in big trouble, resulting in serious, undesirable consequences for all of humanity.

I pepper these analyses with a few of my own experiences. While I know these additions challenge my objective to keep this book short, I hope that the inclusion of these stories will answer some of the questions many people have when they learn about us:

> ➢ Who are we?
> ➢ What are we passionate about?
> ➢ *Why* do we believe what we do?
> ➢ Are we all nuts?

(Spoiler: we're mostly not, but, admittedly, we are motivated and optimistic to a perhaps nutty degree.)

After that, the rest of the book is dedicated to explaining how the empowr platform will leverage each wealth-creating force to create a new web-based Democratic Social Economy— or **DSE**—that will improve the lives of millions of people around our world. Or so we hope.

And finally, we'll wrap up with a discussion on how you can join the effort via a number of avenues, including by easily becoming an empowr citizen and participating in any number of earning roles in the empowr economy, as well as helping some of the world's leading thinkers (in the areas of political science and economics) draft our genuinely democratic—inclusive and participatory—crowdsourced constitution. When we're finished, together we will have created democracy 3.0.

With that laundry list of goals in mind, let's dive into the heart of my message.

HOW DEMOCRACY SAVED THE WORLD

Democracy improved the world by ensuring that leaders aren't left in power so long that they and their cohort become too comfortable or complacent.

By periodically refreshing governments with new people and new ideas, democracy has facilitated many peaceful revolutions that have helped countries worldwide become more prosperous.

Democracy has also created a culture of nonviolent conflict resolution, making international cooperation much easier, and has improved relationships between countries along with the global economy.

On a mild summery morning, a small group of seemingly ordinary men woke up and jumped out of bed. To the casual observer, it appeared to be a morning like any other, as people all over town woke for breakfast and a morning cup of coffee or tea then went about their usual business. But this morning was different; different in a way that would make headlines across the globe. Rather than pack a lunch or grab a drink for the road, *these* unremarkable men awoke and then loaded their backpacks with volatile explosives. They then proceeded to carefully selected destinations and boarded vehicles according to plan, brushing past women, children, and other commuters.

Once in position among the many human beings they had planned for months to murder, each man detonated his explosives. As the bombs' powerful blasts ripped through inanimate objects and innocent people alike, they took a bloody, devastating toll. When the smoke cleared and the shrapnel settled, the lives of many dozens of people had ended violently. One thousand others lay injured.

***Bombing aftermath in London*[2]**

People around the world looked on in shock as their television screens filled once again with acrid smoke, agonized faces, broken bodies, and myriad victims of yet another terror attack. Just a few years before, our world had seen the monstrous new face of modern barbarism. Still, none of us had been truly prepared for the next round of atrocities.

These July 2005 London bombings (often referred to as the 7/7 bombings) were tragic almost beyond words, but they could have been even worse (more people dead and injured) had it not been for the fast action and cooperation between the United States' Central Intelligence Agency (CIA) and empowr's phase 1—code-named "SMS.ac."

SMS.ac

SMS.ac was the very first laboratory stage—or pre-alpha stage—of the project that would grow into empowr. That phase had only two purposes, the first of which was to enable the "economy" part of the **Democratic Social Economy** by inventing a way for people to pay for things electronically over the web. At that time, most web users were "cash and carry": they didn't have credit cards or any other way to pay for things electronically. So, if we couldn't first solve that challenge, there could be no economy or *DSE*—or empowr.com.

One of our many ideas was to convince the world's mobile phone carriers to allow our software to talk to their billing systems, so that people could use their ten-digit phone numbers as if they were credit card numbers. The idea was that charges would show up on their phone bills or be deducted from their pre-paid mobile credit accounts.

The phone companies would not play along, so we needed to find a way to get their attention. We searched endlessly for opportunities or flaws in their business models and technologies, avenues that we might (legally) exploit to get their attention—and grab a seat at their tables.

What we learned was that, when one mobile phone company's customers sent text messages to another phone company's customers, both companies lacked the ability to track and quantify those messages. In other words, if, during any day, the customers of France Telecom sent 100 million text messages to the customers of Deutsche Telekom in Germany, but Deutsche Telekom's customers sent only 95 million text messages back to France Telecom's customers, the phone companies ignored the 5 million difference, and no money changed hands between them because of their inability to successfully track and report that difference to each other.

Once we discovered this flaw, we set out to find a way to gain (legal) access to any *one* phone carrier's text messaging platform and to use that gateway to send text messages to the customers of *other* carriers around the world. The idea was that, if we could do that, we could open up a website and allow users to send text messages from the web to anyone in the world without paying for those messages. The theory was that offering free text messaging to consumers might bring millions of them to our platform via word-of-mouth—since we had no money for marketing—*AND* might give us leverage with the phone companies (in our quest to gain access to their billing systems), because we could show them that we had their customers' attention; attention that we could utilize to help or harm their business objectives.

We spent over two years pursuing this strategy, and, despite our best efforts traveling around the world to meet with phone companies, we always returned home empty-handed.

Having exhausted all our resources, we were on the ropes. In a last gasp attempt, we decided to stop flying out to meet with directors and vice-presidents of phone companies and instead started to dial directly into the offices of the presidents of phone companies around the world, hoping to convince them to board a plane and visit *us*.

That strategy worked! The president of a phone company in South Africa agreed to visit our offices in San Diego, California.

There was only one problem. We had no "offices." We were thirty-five engineers and product professionals working out of my apartment, because we couldn't afford to pay the rent for an office. Surely if that president saw our poor working conditions, there wasn't a chance in hell that he would want any affiliation with our company, much less agree to allow us to connect into his proprietary network.

So we pooled our dollars together and rented a fancy hotel room overlooking the beach, at the famous Hotel Del Coronado in San Diego. When I picked up the president at the airport, I told him that our company was such a big customer of the grand hotel that they were eager to throw rooms at us anytime we needed one, free of charge. So, I said, he and I might as well stop there for discussions before heading over to "our offices."

For our meeting, we had mocked up the designs for a product and made it look like it was almost ready to launch. We discussed our vision for mobile data and the future, and time passed by quickly. At one point, he informed us that he would need to get back to the airport soon and regretted that he wouldn't be able to visit our offices. When I dropped him off at the airport, we agreed with a handshake that his company would allow us to send unlimited text messages, via their platform, to the customers of almost all mobile phone companies around the world. Within a couple of weeks, we both signed a contract to that effect.

A few weeks later, we launched www.SMS.ac—a simple website that allowed people to send free text messages to the mobile phones of their friends anywhere in the world. Given that text messaging was something people were accustomed to paying for, word of mouth exploded instantly, and within six months, over six million mobile customers had signed up—strictly through word of mouth—providing SMS.ac with the fastest customer ramp-up of any company in history (or so we were told). We broke the world records set by Hotmail and Napster, according to *Fast Company* magazine and *USA Today*.

More important than world records and cocktail party stories, we were able to go back to the mobile phone companies and tell them that we were quickly developing relationships with millions of their consumers. And, if they didn't give us access to their billing systems, we would start to provide their competitors with advertising access to those customers.

THAT got their attention. One after another, the mobile phone companies of the world began to give us access to their billing systems, starting in the United Kingdom. They allowed our/their customers to pay for things over the web using only their phone numbers. We were finally on our way to knocking down one of the major hurdles in attaining the *"economy"* part of the DSE (Democratic Social Economy).

It's worth mentioning that, in the process, we also generated many billions of dollars for the phone companies. But, thankfully, since we took the time to patent our invention of transactions over mobile devices, the mobile phone companies awarded us with $150 million (U.S. dollars) for our efforts. This meant that along with enabling global electronic payments—which was a must-have enabler for the DSE—our company also "got funded" without taking a dime from venture capitalists or Wall Street.

This was the second objective of empowr's first phase. Not taking any investor capital was important to us because of the "*democratic*" part of the DSE, which called for, among other objectives, returning most of the company's revenues and profits to our users—whom we call "citizens"—instead of the typical model, where profits belong to, and are extracted out, for the benefit of the shareholders.

Working With the CIA to Save Lives

Within hours of the bombs going off, the CIA reached out to us for information. They wanted the now-dead suicide bombers' text messaging history on our platform so that they could catch any other partners and perpetrators before they escaped or planned a next phase of their attacks.

When the CIA approached us and asked us for help, I had significant reasons not to trust the U.S. government and what they were telling us. (I will explain these soon.) But it was hard to ignore the images on the television and the extreme circumstances of this event. If we didn't cooperate and if those people ended up harming others, I knew we might regret that decision for the rest of our lives.

It turned out that the information we gave to the CIA was critical in helping them detain several suspects quickly and stop future terrorist acts that those suspects had planned. To thank us, the CIA flew one of my co-founders and I out to their headquarters in Langley, Virginia and rolled out the red carpet for us. Along with a comprehensive all-day tour of their facilities plus meetings and dining with some high-ranking officials, we even saw President George H. W. Bush, who once headed up the CIA and just happened to be visiting that day to receive an honor in a special ceremony.

While the end result of helping to stop more terror attacks was spectacular and memorable enough, there was another aspect of this experience that really stuck with me. Throughout all my interactions with the CIA, I noticed a common characteristic: the highest level of professionalism that I have encountered from any organization. For example, regardless of the topic we were discussing, they always had an attentive lawyer present to ensure that nothing they said nor the way that they said it might come off as threatening or intimidating to us. Every single discussion was passed through a filter of "is this appropriate or legal to ask or discuss," which almost always slowed down the process but ensured that the rights of me and my colleagues, as U.S. citizens, were protected.

It takes a lot of motivation, process, and organization to ensure that an effective and well-trained lawyer is present at all times. That was just one sign that these people were professionals. I have never witnessed people more focused on doing their job the right way and with the utmost integrity. After all of my meetings with various CIA staff members, I left with the distinct impression that virtually everyone working at the CIA really believed that they had a sacred responsibility to protect not just their fellow citizens but the other free citizens of the world, as well.

It's important to note that, following that experience, we have had no further interactions with the CIA. As I write this in mid-2015, the CIA and NSA aren't exactly the most popular organizations in the world, partly as a result of the secrets revealed by Edward Snowden about extensive U.S. government monitoring of everyone's communications.

But, following my experience with these consummate professionals and the results that they produced, I was left with a new appreciation for the power of democratic governments to create highly efficient agencies able to reach across the world and cooperate with one another in order to save lives. In fact, one of the best things about democracy is that it *fosters not only the national unity* required to create intricate, complex organizations with global reach but *also international cooperation,* which makes that reach much more useful. It's worth noting that no country with a democratically-elected government has ever gone to war against another democracy. Perhaps that's one of the primary reasons democracies work so well together and have so many mutual interests.

Additionally, democracy has been responsible for some of the most inspiring stories of national success ever told.

A Tale of Two Countries

World War II was the most destructive conflict the planet had ever seen, killing about sixty million people and gutting entire continents. Some of the damage done by the war is still visible to this day, more than half a century after it ended. When the war finally did end, after the development and deployment of the world's first nuclear weapon by the United States, countries that had once allied with one another out of convenience, in order to fight Germany, quickly dissolved their alliances and squared off against one another, developing a conflict that became known as the Cold War.

The two most powerful countries involved in the Cold War conflict, the Soviet Union (U.S.S.R) and the United States, created two huge alliances. The U.S. banded together with many other western nations to create the North Atlantic Treaty Organization (NATO), and the Soviet Union founded the Warsaw Pact with a number of other eastern European nations.

Caught in the middle of this giant international conflict were the people of Germany.

This was because, after the Allies defeated Germany in WWII, Germany was divided into two separate countries. The western half of Germany would, years later, align with NATO, and the eastern half joined the Warsaw Pact nations. While each half of Germany had its own preferred official title, the two countries became known simply as West Germany and East Germany.

Less than five years after the end of World War II, West Germany began to embrace fully various aspects of western governance. The government became refocused on transparent democratic elections and capitalist economic policies, while also forcefully rejecting the communist ideology of its East German neighbor.

In 1949, Konrad Adenauer became the first post-war, democratically-elected chancellor of the German Bundestag (Germany's top legislative body). Despite having been at odds with the British in his role as mayor of British-occupied Cologne, when he became chancellor, Adenauer made a point of developing close ties with NATO.[3]

Additionally, Adenauer pursued a policy of broad economic reforms that focused on free-market ideals and recognition of individual liberties. His policies led West Germany to become one of the most inspiring comeback stories of the twentieth century.

During the *Wirtschaftswunder* (German for "economic miracle"), West Germany became a phoenix that rose from the ashes of the most destructive war in human history and grew into an economic powerhouse, as well as a highly influential international force for good.[4] Adenauer's governmental and economic reforms were so comprehensive and successful that West Germany even went on to join NATO in 1955, allying with world powers that only a decade before had been at war with Germany.

During this time, East Germany evolved in a very different way. Under the yoke of what amounted to Soviet occupation, the country's economy made only a sluggish recovery. Marxist Communism was established, and it led to a great deal of dissatisfaction among East Germans because many of the policies made little economic sense. While the East German government was, in theory, supposed to operate with a great deal of autonomy from the Soviet government, many historians agree that it functioned mostly as a proxy regime for the U.S.S.R.

Private industry was heavily regulated or taken over by the government entirely, which stifled entrepreneurialism. Nearly every other aspect of the economy was directly controlled by the government, as well. On top of this, the Soviet Union extracted billions of dollars' worth of industrial equipment from East Germany as part of war reparations.

Worse, even as they looted East Germany's industry, the Soviets also imposed heavy quotas on all East German production, forcing many workers to put in incredibly long hours. Additionally, the Soviet Union regularly paid a ridiculously small percentage of market value for the goods it bought from East Germany.

Aggravating these predatory economic conditions in East Germany were the restrictions on individual liberties and religious freedoms imposed on citizens by the government. The East German secret police force, known as the Stasi, became renowned for its repressive, ham-fisted tactics.

Often, Stasi officers would detain suspected dissidents and subject them to incredibly harsh interrogation techniques or even outright torture. Over the course of the Cold War, many Stasi detainees disappeared, never to be heard from again. As the Cold War ramped up and the shadowy conflict between NATO and the Warsaw Pact grew uglier each year, East German liberties were even further restricted.

Due to the heavy quotas and restrictions on individual liberties imposed on East Germans, many people (unsurprisingly) fled to West Germany or other countries before the construction of the Berlin Wall in 1961. While the Berlin Wall deserves a book of its own, as it represented perhaps one of the most striking and enduring symbols of the differences between democratic and totalitarian-communist government, I'll just quickly summarize its story.[5]

The city of Berlin was located in East Germany but was in the unique position of being controlled by four different world powers. Divided into quarters, the city was controlled by the U.S., Britain, France, and the Soviet Union.

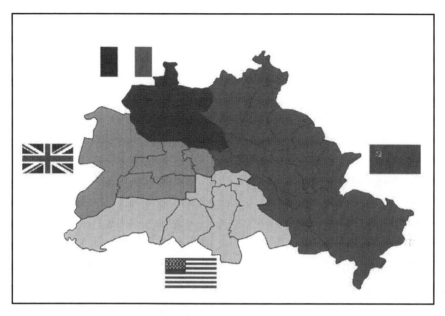

***Berlin Blockade Map (UTC)*[6]**

Since the city was located in East Germany, the East German government and the Soviet Union had a great deal of control over how easily the western powers could supply their people within the city. This created a number of difficulties for the allies. At one point during the Cold War, the Soviet Union even cut off all supply routes to the Berlin's western half, forcing the U.S. and its allies to airlift supplies to West Berlin in an operation that would become known as the Berlin Airlift.[7]

During the Cold War, so many East Berliners tried to escape to the West that the Soviet Union built a huge wall, complete with heavily armed guards, razor wire, and minefields to prevent the exodus. Despite this, the population of East Germany declined from 19 million people in 1948 to only 16 million in 1990. [8] Over time, thousands of East Germans tried to escape over the wall, and hundreds were killed or captured.

The unsuccessful socioeconomic policies and restrictions of individual freedoms imposed on East Germany by the Soviet Union eventually drove a large wedge between the Soviets and the East German people. As a result, after decades of being dominated by Soviet influence, an increasingly independent East German government began to seek a closer relationship with both West Germany and other members of NATO.

Finally, after years of conflict and despite the efforts of the Soviet Union and its proxy, the East German Socialist Unity Party, the Cold War did not turn out in their favor. The flawed economic policies and iron-fisted rule of the Soviet Union combined with the huge costs of the Cold War to bring about the collapse of both its own communist government and many of the puppet regimes it had maintained over the course of the Cold War.

In 1989, the Berlin Wall was opened up, and people began to cross freely between East and West Germany. The wall was soon torn down entirely. In 1990, the two Germanys reunited into one country. This reunification led to a dismantling of communist economic policies and the reinstatement of personal freedoms. The result was a huge increase in per capita GDP in the former East Germany.

***Berlin Wall Comes Down*[9]**

Despite an exponential growth in GDP, there were some downsides to the reunification. Many East Germans lost their jobs, and the homeless count increased as a result. Further, many East German women who had benefitted under socialist rule from great strides toward gender equality found themselves at odds with the male-dominated western economy.[10]

Though some things made reunification less than ideal for a number of East Germans, after a relatively short period of time, the country regained its reputation as one of the most economically important countries in the world. An East German woman, Angela Merkel, even became chancellor of Germany. Now the most powerful economy in the European

Union, Germany's highly efficient democracy, world-class educational system, and thriving technology-driven economy are the envy of many countries across the globe.

The story of the two Germanys is just one of a number of examples of how countries with democratically elected governments have consistently outperformed countries with every other type of government.

The truth is that I could write an entire book on how democracy has saved the world, but, as I said earlier, I'd rather be brief than make you read through pages of evidence. So, since pictures tell a thousand words, here are just a few graphs that demonstrate the huge difference democratic governance can make:

The Koreas

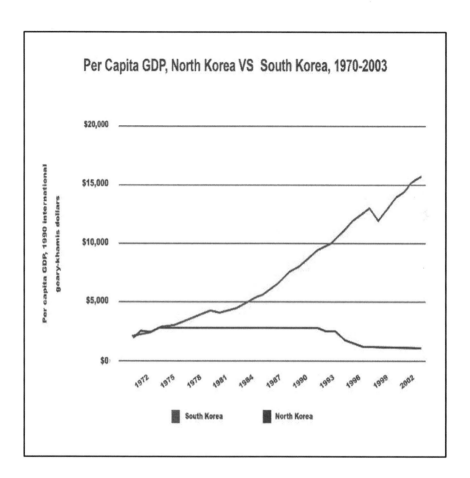

Per Capita GDP, North Korea VS South Korea, 1970-2003

The Germanys

In the following graph, follow the line to see how fast East Germany's GDP rose as a percentage of West Germany's GDP after the fall of the Berlin wall:

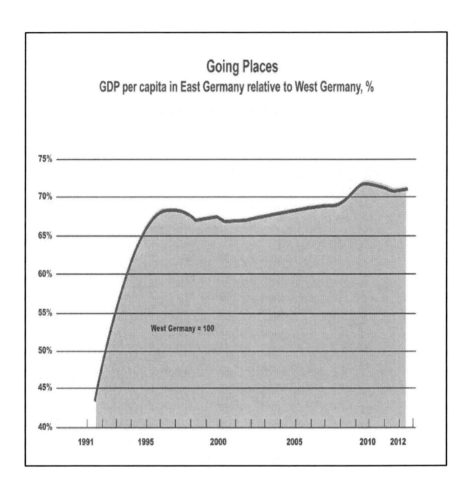

In the following graph, even though the U.S. clearly has the higher per capita GDP...

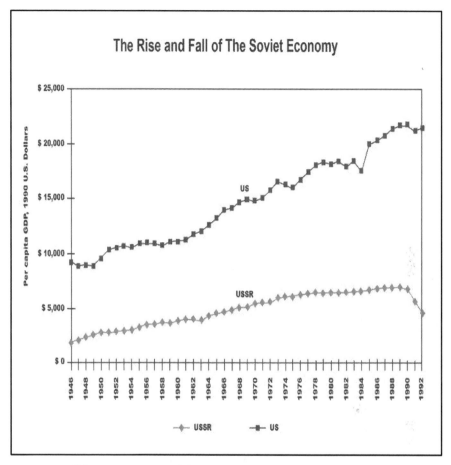

Catching Up Overtaking: USSR v.US GDP, 1946-1992[11]

...upon closer investigation, you can see that the main economic activity of the old USSR was oil production—so their true economic capabilities were even worse than they appear:

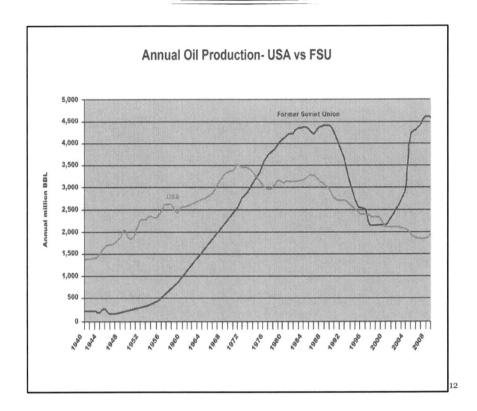

Much has been written about why democracy works better to improve the lives of its citizens. I won't use buzz words like *transparency, accountability,* and *efficiency.* Those concepts also happen to be totally possible under non-democratic systems.

While there are a number of factors in play, it is my opinion that one simple concept is responsible for the *majority* of why democracy works better than other systems. I believe that, if we all understand this simple concept, we'll see why many democracies like our own here in the United States are currently experiencing great difficulty. You'll also gain a deeper insight into why we made certain decisions and utilized specific approaches, as we worked to build our own democratic framework within empowr.com.

The Magic Ingredient

Let me start by telling you a dirty little secret.

I hate (and I mean *really* hate) starting new businesses.

Building a team that works well together is *a lot* harder than it sounds. First, you have to interview tons of people and, after only limited conversation, try to figure out if they have the skills to do the job, skills that you may not even possess yourself.

But, just as important, you need to understand how their values match your own and those of the organization—easier said than done. How will they fit in the culture that you're trying to build? How will they behave in those inevitable times when the going gets tough? People are often quite different in interviews than they are under pressure. How will they really act when it's time to set and achieve goals? Will they accept the pressure of big goals and do whatever is humanly possible to accomplish them? Or will they expend most of their time and energy thinking through how—after missing their goals— they will report that the goals were actually unreasonable and that missing them was not their fault?

Once I put together a team, the long process of teaching them the industry's history begins. Each new member needs to have a working knowledge of what is working and what has been tried but failed, so they can avoid those pitfalls and prevent the company from repeating the same mistakes. Also crucial to the learning curve is the development of a deep understanding as to the reasons why things have failed in the past.

The chemistry between a new team member and the others becomes apparent within weeks. There is very little that can damage the progress of a team or company *more* than having one or more members who turn out to be a bad fit.

Since all experienced managers come with a different set of experiences and each one followed a different path to arrive at this point in his or her career, they usually have many conflicting beliefs about how to approach problems. It usually takes one, two, or even more years to work through those differences. When you buy a new car, they tell you that it will take a while for the engine parts to wear in and work together optimally. It's similar with people: as people get used to working with one another, they learn about everyone's strengths and weaknesses, when to defer to others in a strategic discussion, and when to take the lead.

Along the way, a number of team members will give up and leave or be pushed out as it becomes clear to them and/or others that the conflicts between them are too big to "wear down" comfortably. And so the hiring and interviewing process starts all over again, as does the process of getting everyone on the same page and working well together, once a new person is hired.

And *that's* why it can take many years to get a group of highly skilled and experienced team members to work well together and get some big things done. For me, those are not fun years, but, unfortunately, they're necessary if you want to make magic happen. Steve Jobs says it took him over ten years to achieve that at Pixar, after which the successes started to come one after another, like magic.

Ask the best venture capitalists how they choose businesses to invest in, and they'll invariably tell you that they invest primarily in *the team behind the business*, not the ideas in the business. VCs know how incredibly difficult it is to get a team running like clockwork, so they spend a lot of resources searching for teams that have already reached that magical point; the actual business idea or business model comes in at second place in their investment decision-making process.

Once my team reaches that hard-earned magical point, I have a technology guy, a finance gal, an operations manager, a product person, a top marketing person, head of sales, a general counsel, and a ton of other top-notch professionals in whom I have confidence. When anyone in the entire organization has a new idea or project, they know whom they need to speak with to share that new idea or get those things approved.

Besides the management and employees, the organization also needs outside help to succeed. It requires the assistance of vendors, consultants, advisors, and experts in many fields. Similarly, it takes *a lot* of time and work to establish those relationships and to make them work well, too.

When the entire organization reaches this level of synergy, it's a really good thing. After a while, everybody knows what to expect from everybody else, and which processes and ideas are fair game and which ones aren't. As certain ideas are tried and some work and others fail, the entire organization of human resources—those working inside and outside the company—goes through the experiences together. The organization becomes smarter together, learning what works and what doesn't. It becomes many times more efficient, as everyone benefits from those learnings. They can avoid the mistakes made by others in the organization and also learn from—and add to—the successes. The company vocabulary even changes, with single words or phrases able to communicate a whole strategy that failed or succeeded.

The result is that the success rate for new ideas and projects improves dramatically, and everything can happen much more quickly, as an organization comes alive, similar to how a small child learns to crawl... then walk... then run.

In today's hyper-competitive business environment, to achieve success in a large and desirable market, you usually need to have an organization that operates at that *magical point*. It's quicker and easier to get things done because trust has been built up, and everyone knows all the shorthand terms and unspoken rules. And it's *comfortable,* because the team converges on the same ways of seeing the world that confirm your own.

It is precisely at this *comfortable* point in an organization's evolution that the trouble begins.

The Downside of Comfort

Human nature is to avoid anything that causes discomfort and, from a business perspective, there are few things more painful than failure. This means that teams eventually become resistant to ideas that even slightly resemble other ideas that have failed in the past. On the occasion that new people with new ideas are brought on board, the entire existing team pushes back against any changes the newcomer tries to make to the status quo. Eventually even the most energetic and passionate new hires stop pushing for change or offering new ideas. In order to keep their jobs and fit in, they adapt to the culture of maintaining the status quo, and innovation is stifled even further.

This scenario happens not because people are inherently bad or lazy, but because people are *busy*. When people have very little spare time, they tend to look for the fastest solutions and gravitate toward the paths that offer the least resistance. As more and more members of a team become dependent on predictable, low-effort solutions to their problems and become opposed to new, untested ideas that may result in failure, the entire team settles into a state of comfortable inertia that slowly cripples the entire business.

Further, this settling-in process leads to people staying in jobs they've outgrown or no longer enjoy, simply because they've become so comfortable. Upper-level managers lose their passion for the business and stop seeking out new, more efficient ways to do things. Often, this is not because they are bad people or because they are actively corrupt, but because they have gotten used to things being done a certain way by certain people. In this way, the longer leaders stay in power, the more the system begins to become bogged down with a kind of *passive or* what I call *unintentional corruption*. This soft corruption and laziness trickles down to middle- and lower-level managers who, in turn, also stop finding new ways to motivate and inspire their subordinates.

After a while, this "go with the flow" attitude spreads to the entire organization—even to the other businesses, vendors, agents, and consultants it works with—and the corporation becomes a slow, cumbersome organism moving in one predictable direction. Or, more often, hardly moving anywhere at all.

The result is that all internally vetted ideas become stuck in a certain company mindset. Curiosity, innovation, and the motivation to buck trends are almost all totally squashed. At some point, the entire company becomes unresponsive or even outright hostile to new ideas that might rock the boat or change the direction of the business. Once this stage is reached, inevitably what happens is that a smaller, hungrier, more nimble and innovative company comes along and kicks the big, lazy company's ass.

And finally, when the organization has new projects that absolutely must be started, they are given to the people, vendors, and businesses that are most familiar and comfortable to deal with. When this happens in the organizations that are the governments of countries—which are like corporate organizations in many ways—this is exactly *where unintentional corruption begins*: A government's leadership team innocently starts to give the new projects and their associated budgets to those outside people and firms who are most comfortable to work with. Over time, the companies not receiving new projects shrink in both size and capability. Soon after, the selected companies become the only ones with the infrastructure and resources needed to get the job done, slowly solidifying themselves as the only choice for future projects.

Without competition, these companies become inefficient and lethargic and, as a result, must charge the government higher prices to get the same job done. Little by little, those countries' infrastructure, schools, and economies stagnate, as progress slows to an almost complete halt. And wealth and power accumulate in the hands of a smaller and smaller group of people (the people who own those large and lethargic companies).

To fully understand the problem of corruption, how innocently it starts and how difficult it is to remove, imagine one little (or big) kingdom. The King's (or President's or Prime Minister's or Chairman's or *insert your favorite ruler title here*) wife's brother's son-in-law gets an exclusive license to import fancy mattresses (mostly used in hotels, since local people are too poor to buy them) and earns a nice living doing so, free from competitors.

Eventually some motivated entrepreneur comes along and says, "You know, if this other person is earning monopoly prices importing fine mattresses, then I'll just manufacture some here domestically." But that entrepreneur is naive. The exclusive import license wasn't an accident, as it reflects the ruler's wife's brother's son-in-law's special relationship within the political system. Smart hotel operators will know better than to purchase mattresses from the new competitor, since to do so will bring them regulatory problems. Intelligent bankers will know that the new business will fail and won't lend the entrepreneur money, and, even if it doesn't fail, lending him capital will bring them regulatory problems, too. Eventually, the new entrepreneur's smart wife will explain to him why his business idea is doomed.

Without opportunity, both people and money stagnate, and the smartest people instead focus their energies on ascending the ladder of corruption. Even if the ruler finally comprehends that, on some level, he's helped create a counterproductively corrupt system, he soon realizes that, if he starts threatening the income streams of the folks he depends on to support the regime, his own base will disappear.

Now apply our little mattress example to hundreds or thousands of other products and services, and you'll start to understand the web of power, revenue relationships, and dependencies that quickly and permanently form, *extracting* significant opportunities out of the economy and away from its citizens. Once it gets going, it's hard to untangle the giant web of corruption.

◆◆◆

But I digress. Let's go back to our big hypothetical company, where our company was about to get its ass kicked. Imagine that the entire group of people at the top of this giant business is walking back to work after lunch and they're all hit by a bus. (Don't worry, none of them felt a thing.) Let's also pretend that nobody within the organization is qualified to replace the dearly departed management team. Suddenly, the shareholders have to find new people to run the business. In comes an entirely new management team who are all excited about their new roles. With them come new ideas and a passion for making the company succeed in fresh, innovative ways.

The new management is so amped about their new jobs that they don't just passively let new ideas float in; they actively seek them out. As the new bosses take over, their excitement trickles down throughout the entire organization. The other members of the team either rediscover their own passion for their jobs (and the drive to try new ideas that comes with that passion) or they are replaced with new people who have that critical energy. As a result of all this, the giant company becomes more agile and innovative, and it also has the resources to challenge any smaller competitors that try to compete with it.

As many new ideas are tried, some succeed, and that builds momentum and motivation to try even more new ideas. It's true that human beings don't like the discomfort associated with failing, but it's also true that they love the feeling of victory, so, for a while, new ideas are sought out and chased with full vigor—like a drug addict looking for his next fix. Ideas and passion are the seeds of creative destruction and reconstruction.

It turns out that the unfortunate bus incident turned out to be a really good thing for our hypothetical company. Perhaps nothing else but losing the entire management team all at once could have turned this organization around and made it responsive and alive, efficient and able to serve its customers again.

The governments of countries are like corporate organizations in many ways. They are the largest and most powerful organizations in the world, tasked with the serious business of running countries. In an ideal world, democratic elections in countries are less dramatic versions of the bus that hit our hypothetical company's management team. Elections facilitate what I like to think of as "peaceful revolutions," when different people with fresh new ideas are promoted to lead the country, replacing the old leaders and their web of relationships—hopefully before too much intentional and unintentional corruption has had time to materialize—so that new approaches to old problems can be formulated and acted on with new passion, vigor and excitement.

The peaceful revolutions that democratic elections bring revitalize governments from the top down. This allows governments to adapt to new world conditions and grow with the country and the people they are responsible for governing. In turn, things move faster within the government. As old, inefficient relationships end, the entire organization—from top politicians all the way down to the lowest level government contractor—can come alive and have an infinitely higher chance of doing a better job taking care of the peoples' needs in an honest, focused, and efficient way.

It's this last part—the regular ousting of the old guard and the bringing in of new, passionate, and creative leaders—that I believe is the most vital part of a successful democracy. It is exactly that concept, more than anything else, that makes democracies work better than any other system in the long run. Unfortunately, it is this absolutely critical element of the democratic process that has been hurt or even destroyed outright in some democracies, including here, in the United States.

...DEMOCRACY IS BROKEN

In recent decades, the peaceful revolution that is so important to the long-term success of democratic governments and those countries they serve has been hijacked by special interests. No longer is the old guard being replaced with fresh new faces who bring vigor and passion to their work.

Rather, many democratic governments are now completely beholden to powerful groups within their country, which bankroll politicians' campaigns in an effort to keep things exactly the way they are, because the status quo is already making these groups rich beyond belief.

This has left many democracies unable to respond to the needs of the countries and people they govern or to the global challenges that the past century has presented.

It was 2 a.m., and I was sleeping in my office parking lot with my head resting on a moldy pillow. Next to me were several Chevy vans stuffed with envelopes containing many millions of dollars. As a tech entrepreneur, this was most definitely *not* what I'd had in mind when I'd started the business. The story leading up to my night of parking lot van babysitting is a case study in how government can go wrong, and how the democratic process has been damaged over the past few decades.

I was running my very first company after dropping out of college, and it had taken off very quickly. The basic idea was relatively simple: we helped students find scholarships and grants on the Internet.

Back in those days, searching the Internet (called Arpanet at the time) was a much more complex operation. Computers were more expensive, worked many times slower, and rarely connected to a network. So, to find scholarships on the Internet, students would send in their search request along with a sixty-dollar check, and we would key their search into our computers, scour the Internet, print the results, and send them back to them.

By developing software-based information crawlers, we had automated the process of trolling the computers of university financial aid offices and had amassed a large database of financial aid sources, similar to the way Google crawls the Internet today to build its search database.

As soon as our database was packed with hundreds of thousands of sources of financial aid, we gave students at my university (University of California, San Diego) first pass at it. Word of mouth exploded on that campus. Within weeks, word had spread to neighboring colleges. Only two months after launching, requests for our services were coming in from virtually every other college and university around the nation. To the best of my knowledge, this was the first commercially successful Internet search business.

Unaccountable Government and Runaway Bureaucracy

Unfortunately for us, the United States Postal Service became alarmed at the exploding number of envelopes that we were receiving each day and the amount of money they contained. This resulted in the Postal Service essentially holding our company hostage by seizing our mail and revenues, making it impossible for us to pay the rent or even make payroll. Our only option was to take up the case in federal court, in essence suing the federal government in its own courtrooms—a daunting task for a twenty-one-year-old with only a few months' business experience who had never even seen the inside of a courtroom.

My lawyers advised me not to fight the case, given that a staggeringly high percentage of these types of cases are won easily by the government. But, in my almost naive belief in the U.S. justice system, I couldn't fathom being taken advantage of in such a way without putting up a fight.

I will never forget the answer the prosecutor gave to the federal judge when asked why the Post Office had taken the action in the first place, and how many complaints they were responding to. "No," he said. "There weren't any complaints from customers. But, in our experience, when a company is doing this well this fast, they must be doing something wrong."

It was then that I fully realized that not only was I being unjustly prosecuted by the government, but the people who were pursuing the case were doing so because, in their eyes, my business was simply too successful.

The United States government was too powerful and out of control.

On a quick side note, my attorney in this case also suggested that the investigators were probably quite happy to be in the city of San Diego at the time of year that our hearing took place. American East Coast cold is no joke, and it may well have been possible that a taxpayer-funded vacation to America's finest city was just too tempting to pass up. Obviously, it's just a theory..., but it does serve to give you an idea of how bad potential governmental abuse of power can be when there is no proper oversight by responsible elected officials. But I digress.

Long story short: in large part because of expert testimony from the University of California, San Diego (UCSD)'s Director of Financial Services Thomas Rutter, the judge ruled in our favor and ordered the Postal Service to release our mail and money. By that time, mountains of envelopes had accumulated containing checks that totaled, cumulatively, many millions of dollars. There were so many envelopes that we needed several large vans to transport them from the Postal Office to the bank. Since the bank just closed for the weekend, my business partner and I, along with some of our employees, had to take turns sleeping in the vans to make sure they didn't disappear before Monday, along with all the money they contained.

I had been incredibly fortunate. If it weren't for UCSD's Thomas Rutter's ability to really understand what our software was doing, plus his belief that the American justice system ultimately could reach the right conclusion, I probably would have lost. And if the federal judge hadn't decided to allow me to bring in and connect up all my computers in her courtroom and hadn't actually come down from her bench to sit in front of them and patiently learn what my software did—which was unprecedented at the time and occurred over the many objections of the government prosecutors—I surely would have lost.

In addition, if my 200 employees hadn't believed in the company enough to stick around, even though they were not being paid during those few months when our money was held captive by the government, there would have been no company to come back to after winning. And *that's* how powerful the government is: even in the slight chance that they lose, they still succeed at their objective of breaking the people and businesses they pursue.

In fact, just a few days after winning the case, I ended up resigning from my company. I didn't shut it down, because I wanted the employees that had believed and waited so patiently to still have their jobs, but I simply handed my share of the company to my co-founder—for free—and walked away with only a promise that he would be kind to the employees. Sure, I was exhausted but perhaps more importantly, I was disgusted by what I had learned about the system and government that I had believed in with all my heart. I needed time to rethink what had happened before I could care again to muster up the energy to do anything in America – including live in it. You see, I was *in love with America,* and now I felt violated and betrayed, like I imagine one would feel when they first find out that their lover had cheated on them.

After having a chance to get some distance from the whole experience, it wasn't hard to conclude that America had not betrayed me. Even though I had been unjustly persecuted and bullied by the United States government, America had ultimately—through its quite purposely separated and independent judicial system—kept its promise.

I decided that what I should do, instead of becoming bitter or jaded, is use my talents and energies to double-down on the concept of America and do my part to help correct its injustices.

Years later, out of curiosity, I reached out to the government investigator who had been responsible for starting the investigation. He apologized and admitted that they'd been "overzealous" in pursuing their case against us. Having a talent for understatement is, apparently, a prerequisite for a job with the government.

In any case, I try not to hold grudges, so I look at the entire thing as water under the bridge. That said, I do think the story provides a good example of why and how systems that are supposed to be democratic have become bogged down by their own bloated weight over the past few decades.

I don't really blame the postal investigators for initiating the investigation. My company received amounts of money in the mail that grew exponentially, and I can totally understand how it might have looked suspicious. But when it found no evidence of wrongdoing, including and especially no unhappy customers, the government should have ended the investigation and let me go back to running my business. Instead, because of American democracy's increasing inability to create "peaceful revolutions" at the top, the U.S. government poured tons of taxpayer dollars into a case that, early on, they had already figured out had no foundation.

One other very important thing that my experience with the government taught me: *you should <u>never</u> back down from a fight if you believe your cause is just.* No matter how powerful the person or organization you're going up against is, you should you always stick to your guns. If your intention is to improve the world in some way, you will invariably face the very forces that have worked to keep it the way that it currently is.

This philosophy has helped me countless times throughout my professional life and has been a huge part of the success I've been fortunate enough to find. In fact, without learning this vital lesson, I would never have been able to build empowr and assemble the team capable of creating the Democratic Social Economy that powers it.

David and Goliath

Unfortunately for everybody, once organizations within governments get going in a certain direction, it's nearly *impossible* for them to adjust course even slightly, let alone change course entirely. After the investigators started the investigation, they became slaves of a system that insisted they throw a crazy amount of resources at it, in order to justify their case against us. The system expected things to be done a certain way; the way that they had been done for decades, because of a lack of shake-ups at the top. And I bet that, if anybody involved in the investigation had tried to stop it, they would have been hung out to dry by their coworkers and superiors for endangering the case and the huge budget expenditures it had generated.

The government agency needs its budget to keep running, and, if it can be demonstrated that the organization wasted money on frivolous lawsuits, their budget is likely to be cut. So, by winning cases like this at any cost, they are "proving" that they are doing things right and saving themselves from both budget cuts and embarrassment.

In much the same way, the democratic process has been hijacked in a number of countries around the world. Politicians in a number of the world's democracies are required to raise huge sums of money in order to run the campaigns they need to be elected to political office. While the most expensive campaigns are typically for national office, even state and local elections are becoming something that only people who start out wealthy (or who are successful at enlisting wealthy backers) can ever hope to afford.

Depending on the length of their terms, this phenomenon means that politicians are forced to spend far too much of their time in office worrying about how they are going to pay for their reelection campaign and not nearly enough time figuring out ways to fix the country's problems. This is evidenced by the ridiculous amount of "pork" attached to many pieces of new legislation. Pork is just a succinct way of saying that a politician involved in the writing of a bill added something to it that ensured his political backers got a few vanloads of taxpayer dollars thrown their way.

As with the investigators from the U.S. government, I don't blame individual politicians themselves for worrying more about getting reelected than about doing their jobs once they're in office. Many democratic systems have been corrupted to the point where the people who run them are absolutely required to kowtow to the needs of special vested interests if they want to stand any chance of rising to or staying in political office.

Even worse, on the rare occasion that a politician is elected without leasing her political career to big money and then tries to change the way the system works, she is attacked from all sides by her colleagues *and* by the special interests who make a killing maintaining the status quo. For an example, let's look to my home country, the United States.

Endangered Democracy and the Rise of the Post-industrial Oligarch

In the U.S., only a couple thousand companies have $1 billion of yearly revenue. Thanks to the erosion of campaign finance laws (which used to limit how much money these companies can give politicians), these 2,000 or so companies have a much larger say in the direction of political discourse within the United States than the vast majority of the American people. This is because politicians (especially those seeking national office) know that, in order to get elected and pursue their political agenda, they have absolutely no choice but to keep happy these couple thousand companies plus a number of billionaires and a group of special interests with big budgets. If they do so, they can afford the television ads required to get the vote. If they don't, they won't be reelected. Unfortunately, it really is that simple.

As a result of this warped democratic process, the peaceful revolutions that our elections used to usher in have become things of the past. Here in the U.S. (a shining example of democracy that is looked to by a lot of the world—or used to be...), we are now electing (and re-electing again and again and again) politicians who have no business being in public office. This happens to a large degree because, at one point in time, elected officials decided to make it easier to stay in power by attacking term limits (i.e., how many times they can run for reelection) and by rolling back campaign finance reforms. Because of this, the same stagnation that occurs within corporations that don't introduce peaceful revolutions at the top (the ones that bring in new people, ideas, and passion) is also occurring within the government of the United States.

As a consequence, the great effects of a vibrant, thriving democracy that we once enjoyed here in the States are disappearing. Here are just a few examples:

- Since the U.S.'s most recent economic recovery began, roughly 95% of the new wealth created has gone to the top 1% of income earners.[13]

- The United States now has more people in jail, per capita, than any other country in the world—even more than the most repressive regimes on the planet.[14]

- Since 1990, the cost of living within our country has jumped over 55% while the purchasing power of the minimum wage has risen only by roughly 19%.[15]

- U.S. roads, bridges and other public infrastructure are crumbling, with investment down to less than .5% GDP behind Australia's 1.25% and nine other developed nations.[16]

- The U.S educational system, once among the top in the world, is now in 14th place and falling, according to Pearson's Global Education Index.

- Americans spend double the amount per capita on healthcare as other first-world nations, while at the same time our country ranks near the bottom of the industrialized world when it comes to preventing avoidable deaths through timely, effective medical care.[17]

- Satisfaction with national government is at a near all-time low, hovering between 10% and 20%, depending on whom you ask and what branch is being discussed.[18]

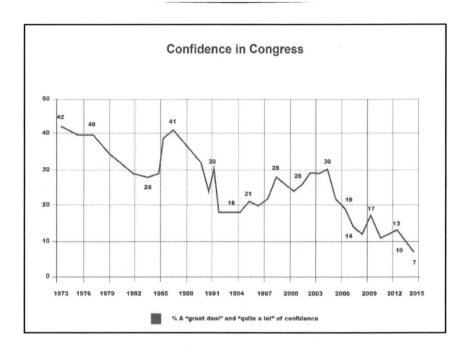

Confidence in Congress

% A "great deal" and "quite a lot" of confidence

- During the late 19th and through the 20th century, the average years of service for Senators has increased steadily, from an average of just under five years in the early 1880s to an average of just over thirteen years in recent Congresses.

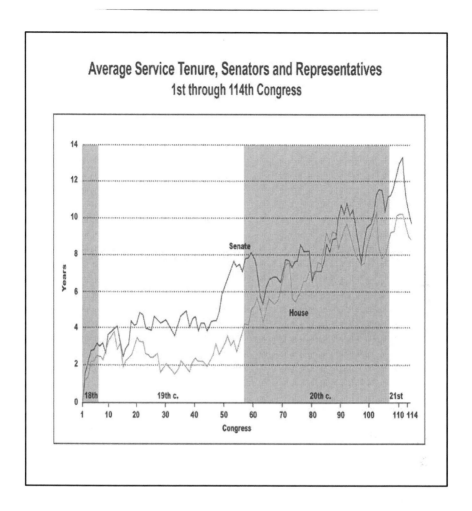

Average Service Tenure, Senators and Representatives
1st through 114th Congress

- Similarly, the average years of service of Representatives has increased from just over four years in the first two Congresses of the 20th century to an average of approximately ten years in the three most recent Congresses.

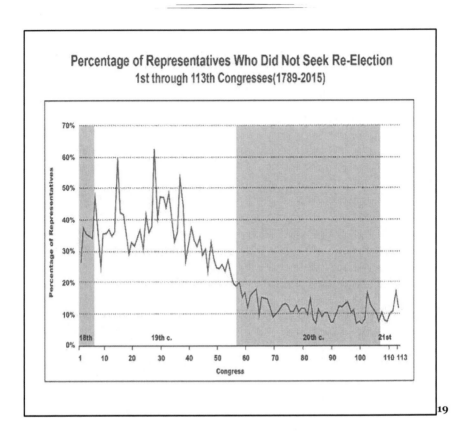

Given the public's almost complete lack of confidence in congress, you might be shocked to know that the reelection rate of congressmen has never dropped below 80% for the past half century for our House of Representatives and has averaged over 80% for our Senate in the past thirty years.

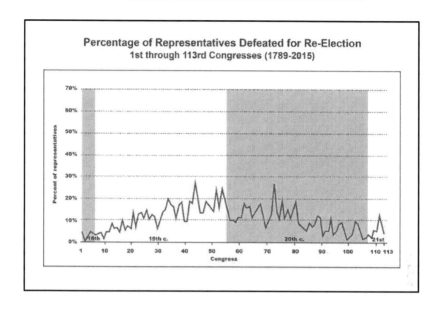

If almost all the people don't like their representatives but those representatives almost always get reelected, it doesn't take a genius to conclude that the people have lost control of their government, which means calling it a democracy is inaccurate.

Once again, I don't think it's the fault of the individual politicians for doing what they need to do in order to be reelected. No matter how noble a politician's ideals, if they can't get elected and retain their office, they can't do a damned thing other than complain.

However, this phenomenon of the constant reelection of politicians who comprise a government that the vast majority of voters disapprove of is a symptom of a broken democratic system that needs to change if it expects to survive. John F. Kennedy once said, "Those who make peaceful revolution impossible will make violent revolution inevitable."

Around the world, democracy is in greater danger than any time in recent history.

The news from Eastern Europe and the Soviet Union in the 1990's, the fall of the Berlin Wall, those were a time when the march of democracy and freedom in the world seemed inevitable. Every time you opened up a newspaper, you expected to see another country opening its arms to freedom.

And today? The trend is leaning in the opposite direction. Recently the watchdog group Freedom House released its annual report on freedom and democracy around the world. It analyzed nearly 200 countries, based on the United Nation's declaration of human rights. They concluded that democracy is in greater danger than anytime in the last 25 years, with 36% of the world's population not being free, 24% partly free, and 40% free.

According to their report, democracy has been declining for the last decade. In 2014, 61 countries saw their freedom decline and 33 saw their freedom improve, the worse showing in over ten years.

If you look at the 21st century overall, freedom has peaked, according to Freedom House. The least free area of the world is Africa and the Middle East, where 85% of the population is not free. The exception is Tunisia—which just a decade ago, had one of the most tyrannical governments in the world.

Dictatorship is on the rise, and its nature is changing— they're no longer even pretending to be democratic. Russia's invasion of Crimea is the most noticeable example. China is arresting activists more than ever and now even televising their confessions.

In Egypt the military has taken over and the courts sentenced hundreds of political prisoners to be executed in fake trials.

There are a good number of dictatorships such as Ethiopia, Azerbaijan and Vietnam, which have managed to avoid the Western media's attention but are just as oppressive.

It's not all bad news, with the Ukrainians revolting against their government despite Russian efforts—and we've also seen some very interesting resistance to oppression in Hong Kong.

The bottom line is that at the end of the cold war, it appeared for a moment that freedom was an unstoppable force, but every force has an undercurrent and perhaps that's what we're seeing these days.

◆◆◆

At empowr, we are huge believers in the power of democracy. Even though it has some serious challenges, it absolutely can be fixed. In the fifteen years that we've been working on empowr, hardly a few days passed where we weren't thinking about and discussing the news, the issues as we saw them and what we could do, as concerned citizens and technologists, to make a difference. More importantly, we have spent all of those years designing, coding, and integrating dozens of interconnected technologies with the objective of making a difference in the direction and future of democracy. If we don't try to help in the only way we can, then we, too, can't do a damned thing other than complain.

One critical way we can make peaceful revolutions possible again is by helping voters understand that their democracy is dying and that its only hope for survival is to impose limits on how many terms any politician may serve, as well as on how much money any single person or entity can give them or spend directly or indirectly on their election campaigns.

The most successful way this has been done in the past is by enabling every citizen to have affordable access to a world-class education—an absolutely essential part of ensuring that democracy endures.

EDUCATION SAVED THE WORLD...

As the industrial revolution kicked off in the mid-1700s, affordable, accessible quality public education became increasingly important to the world. The world population increase, GDP, productivity, and the advancement of every technological field benefitted from this phenomenon. Ultimately, improved public education has helped much of humanity live longer, happier, healthier lives.

"*We don't need no education!*" At least, that's what the song said as I listened to it in my classroom. It was my freshman year of high school, and I was stuck in a French class in which I had *absolutely* no interest. I made my disinterest glaringly apparent to my French teacher by blasting Pink Floyd's "Another Brick in The Wall" during class on one memorable day. For those not familiar with the song, it basically accuses schools of brainwashing students and turning them into drones for society—sort of like simple bricks in a wall. Not the most inspiring song to be listening to as I began my high school education.

As I sat in class, smirking at my French teacher while he scowled down at me, a big vein in his forehead pulsing, I thought I was the funniest kid in school. I had been a rebellious student since the beginning of the semester, but it appeared that Pink Floyd and I had finally pushed my teacher over the edge. He grabbed me by the arm, stood me up, walked me to the empty classroom next door, and forcefully sat me down.

At this point, I was pretty sure I was going to get reamed. You know, the typical threats about the principal's office, calling my parents, that sort of thing. But that day my teacher had something entirely different in mind. With a look that combined extreme annoyance with resignation, he told me that, so long as I stayed in the empty classroom next door for the entire rest of the semester during French class and didn't disrupt the other students' learning, I could do whatever I wanted and he would still give me an "A" in the class.

I thought I was getting the deal of the century! I got to sit and listen to my music *and* I didn't have to put up with any useless, boring French lessons; all while still getting a great grade in the class. Since I didn't like French and I flat out *hated* French class, I quickly agreed to my teacher's offer and spent French period for the rest of the semester listening to music and screwing around in the empty classroom next door. At the time, I thought it was a great arrangement.

But here's the thing, my French is *terrible* now. If my teacher back in high school could have found a way to reach me and help me to understand how awesome it can be to know another language, I might actually be able to speak at least passable French today. I was a cocky, cynical teenager who was a giant pain in the ass for my teachers, but I remember that some of my best teachers were still able to reach me and help me learn the subjects that make me the (arguably) well-rounded person I am today. Without that solid educational foundation, I would probably never have been able to build the companies I've built or develop the new technologies I've been a part of creating.

And that's really the point of this whole story.

The Difference that Great Teachers and Quality Education Make

The best teachers and educational systems *never* give up on providing their students with the highest quality education that's available, whether those students are cooperative and friendly, or they're snot-nosed little jerks like I was. This is because, over the past few hundred years, the world has realized that ensuring the next generation is educated is one of the best ways to safeguard the future of a country. Top-notch teachers and the educational systems they are a part of are one of the cornerstones on which every industrialized nation has been built. President Franklin D. Roosevelt even went so far as to say, "Democracy cannot succeed unless those who express their choice are prepared to choose wisely. The real safeguard of democracy, therefore, is education."

The global recognition that an affordable quality education is critical to a country's success is something that is taken for granted today. Nobody believes a country can get away with having a terrible educational system and still expect to remain globally competitive for very long. But this wasn't always the case. Despite the invention of the printing press in 1439, which made books exponentially more affordable to produce, up until the 18th century, education was often restricted to a relatively small portion of the population. The best that most regular people could hope for was to find a good trade master to whom they could apprentice.

While the start of the industrial revolution in the mid-1700s began to push countries toward educating enough people to invent, produce, and run new machines, it wasn't until the mid-1800s that the model of affordable, quality public education we have today really started to become popular. New national leaders created quality public school systems that were free (or at least very affordable) for everyone, regardless of their status in society. In addition to improving access to education, modern educational systems increased the quality of the material being taught by establishing schools dedicated to training top-notch, professional teachers and professors.

As a result of these educational reforms and the new technologies being produced by the industrial revolution, the world experienced some of the most rapid growth in the history of humanity, as death rates plummeted and birth rates did not. For example, up until the early 18th century, the population of the world had remained under 1 billion people. Yet, as a result of educational reforms and the inventions of the new generations of engineers and scientists that those reforms inspired, the world population jumped from under 1 billion people in the year 1800 to over *6 billion people* in the year 2000.

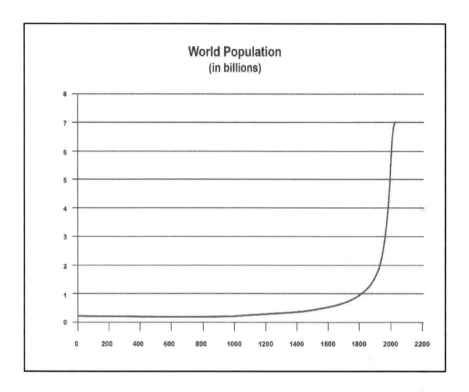

Another example of a benefit of improved public education is how much longer people started to live, once educational reform began. Between 1500 and 1800, the average life expectancy of a regular European is estimated at forty years of age. Thanks to advancements in medicine, sanitation, and health care (particularly reductions in infant mortality) produced by educational reforms, the average life expectancy has now more than *doubled,* with the average European born in 2014 expected to live an incredible eighty-one years. This spectacular growth spurt for humanity was made possible by the industrial, societal, and technological advances created by highly educated people.

Educated People and the Wonders They Created

Many of the most fantastic contributions that have been made to the world were invented or discovered by highly-educated people. Bernard of Chartres, a famous 12th century philosopher and scholar, once wrote that modern people are much like dwarves perched on the shoulders of giants. What he was trying to get at is that, because of those who came before us who learned so much, we can now advance so much further than we ever could have done without their accumulated knowledge.

Because education gives us the ability to stand on the shoulders of giants, it has, over the course of history, led to inventions that revolutionized the world. For instance, take the case of Waldemar Haffkine, a famous Russian doctor and creator of the first vaccines for cholera and the black plague. Born in 1860, Haffkine was educated as a child in Berdyansk, a city in what is now Ukraine.

He attended Malorossiisky University in Odessa, where he studied microbiology and had a chance to work with future Nobel laureates. He eventually earned his doctorate and went on to work at the Louis Pasteur Institute in Paris.[20] It was there, in 1892, that he developed a vaccine for cholera, a disease that was creating regular pandemics throughout the world.[21]

Eventually, Haffkine created a vaccine for the bubonic plague, a disease that had once wiped out almost a quarter of humanity.[22] Haffkine was also a brave man, testing out his vaccines on himself before trying them on other human beings.

Speaking of vaccines, no discussion of them would be complete without including the creator of the polio vaccine, Jonas Salk. The son of poor Jewish immigrants, Salk's intelligence was recognized early on, and at age thirteen he was allowed to attend Townsend Harris High School, a school for gifted children. The public high school prepared him well to attend City College of New York, which charged no tuition but gave him the education he needed to pursue his dream of becoming a doctor.[23]

Salk attended medical school and graduated as a medical doctor. Many years later, he contributed to creating a flu vaccine for the U.S. Army and, in 1957, created the world's first vaccine for polio. In the U.S. alone, polio was killing thousands of people each year and crippling many thousands more. After Salk created the vaccine, it was widely distributed worldwide, saving hundreds of thousands of lives.

Most, if not all, vaccines were created by highly dedicated and highly *educated* medical professionals who learned from the experience and hard work of their predecessors. Thus, without education, millions of people throughout the world would be either dead or horribly crippled by terrible diseases. To get a small idea of the difference that vaccines have made in the United States alone, just take a look at this comparison:

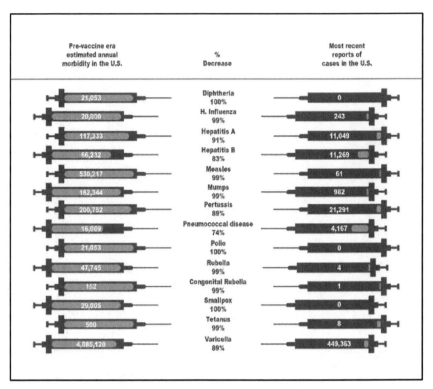

Pre-vaccine era estimated annual morbidity in the U.S.	% Decrease	Most recent reports of cases in the U.S.
21,053	Diphtheria 100%	0
20,000	H. Influenza 99%	243
117,333	Hepatitis A 91%	11,049
66,232	Hepatitis B 83%	11,269
530,217	Measles 99%	61
162,344	Mumps 99%	982
200,752	Pertussis 89%	21,291
16,069	Pneumococcal disease 74%	4,167
21,053	Polio 100%	0
47,745	Rubella 99%	4
152	Congenital Rubella 99%	1
29,005	Smallpox 100%	0
500	Tetanus 99%	8
4,085,120	Varicella 89%	449,363

Vaccine infographic created by Leon Farrant

While vaccines *are* wonderful, they're just one of the fantastic advances brought on by the power of modern education. The number of discoveries and inventions made by highly educated people is countless, but here are a few more, just in case you're not already convinced.

If you're reading this on a computer, chances are you have education to thank for it, especially so if the computer is using a Windows operating system. Microsoft founder Bill Gates graduated from Lakeside School, a top American high school, in 1973 before going on to Harvard, one of the most prestigious universities in the world, where he continued his pursuit of computer science.

One of the most popular misconceptions about Gates is that he didn't need education to succeed but rather did everything on his own. Gates laid this myth to rest in a recent interview when he said, "Although I didn't complete my degree, I was very close. I didn't leave school because I was bored or because I didn't see the value in completing my education. I left because I believed we had a small window of opportunity to launch Microsoft. But, since that time, I have certainly taken a lot of college courses—either online or on DVD. It's one of my favorite things to do—so I'd have to be described as an enthusiast when it comes to higher education."[24]

To further demonstrate Gates's enthusiasm for education, one need look only at the work that the charity he and his wife created is doing across the globe. The Bill and Melinda Gates Foundation spends millions of dollars every year on philanthropy aimed at improving global access to affordable, high-quality education.

The value of education is not limited to technical fields, either. Some of the world's most famous and admired people have been dedicated advocates of education. World renowned South African hero Nelson Mandela once said, "Education is the most powerful weapon which you can use to change the world."[25]

Mandela himself made extraordinary efforts to pursue his own education, even attending college at a time when doing so was extremely difficult for black South Africans.

Another widely respected activist and peacemaker, Mahatma Gandhi, recognized how critical education was to the success of a country, although he thought that teaching through doing was the key to educational success. Gandhi once said, "The real system of education is one where the children of rich and poor, of king and subject, receive education through crafts."[26] One of the lesser-known facts about Gandhi is that he was an English-trained barrister (the English term for lawyer).

The long and short of all of this is that regardless which aspect of modern life you look at, education has played a critical role in making it possible at some point. From constitutions and laws written by highly educated intellectuals to scientific advancements made by doctors who spent *years* in school honing their minds—without widespread, affordable, quality education, the modern world would simply not exist.

By giving huge swaths of humanity access to public schools staffed by well-paid, respected, high-quality teachers, countries around the world have done their very best to prepare students to participate in the growing global economy and in the governments responsible for running those countries. The entire human race has benefitted from the new technologies and ideas that this strategy of universal education produced.

The most important defining aspects of the modernization of global education were *accessibility, quality,* and *affordability.* And it's the rapid reduction in these aspects that now threatens the success of some industrialized nations.

...EDUCATION IS BROKEN

Many first-world educational systems are now in decline. In some countries, schools are finding it nearly impossible to recruit quality teachers, with many teachers coming from the bottom 30% of college graduates. This leads to a nasty cycle, where bad teachers fail to teach students effectively, and those weak students then go on to be bad teachers, themselves, leading to a "dumbification" of entire generations.

Combine this dumbification cycle with a lack of educational transparency which makes it very difficult for students to predict the value of potential degrees, and you begin to see why modern educational systems are in jeopardy.

It was my senior year of college, and I was absolutely miserable. As I sat in class, listening to my professor drone on in a thickly-accented monotone about a programming language that had been obsolete since before I even went to high school, I slowly began to zone out and think back to why I'd come to college in the first place...

After high school, I'd gone straight to the University of California, San Diego (UCSD) to pursue my bachelor's degree in computer science. Being the giant geek that I was, I was very excited about the prospect of a higher education that taught me even more about computer science. I had thought that my college courses were not only going to teach me new, cutting-edge technical skills but that they were also going to allow me to work with professors who were as passionate about innovation and technology as I was.

What I found, instead, were college courses that were years behind the times, and professors who were more concerned with their research projects than with teaching and mentoring the next generation of tech entrepreneurs.

Adding to my frustration was the fact that nobody I spoke with, either on the faculty or in university administration, seemed to be able to explain to me what the hell was going on. No matter how many times I asked, I couldn't get a straight answer as to why the courses were so outdated or how a professor made it through the interview and selection process without even being able to speak basic, understandable English.

The complete lack of accountability and the unwillingness of anyone within the system to take responsibility for addressing obvious, basic problems with the school were astounding...

Sitting there in class, my mind snapped back to the present. The professor was still tonelessly reciting her lecture while seemingly oblivious to the fact that she had lost the entire class long ago. And then, I suddenly made my final decision. I would not waste another minute of my time or another dollar of my money on classes and professors that had no value to me. I stood up, walked out of class, and dropped out of college. I went on to start my first business the very next day...

◆◆◆

To this day, many years after I first went to college, there is still very little accountability for professors; it continues to be nearly impossible to fire a tenured professor (or teacher). This same lack of accountability applies to institutions. Many of them don't even bother to keep track of how well their graduates do after leaving school or whether their curriculums even come close to preparing graduates for the challenges of 21st century business.

Schools are in Crisis

My college story is not unlike what many other U.S. and international college students go through every day. In fact, many young people seeking higher education have it far worse than I did from a number of perspectives.

Here in the U.S., things have gotten particularly bad for college students. While there has only been some slow, incremental progress in updating curriculums to keep pace with the needs of our post-industrial economy, tuition hikes since I attended college have been neither slow nor incremental.

In fact, tuition and college-associated fees in the United States have skyrocketed an astounding 1,120% since we started keeping records back in 1978. [27] No, I didn't accidentally let an extra 1 slip by. That *really* says one thousand, one hundred and twenty percent. This mind blowing spike in tuition means that, this year, the average four-year-college graduate here in the States will leave school almost $30,000 in debt.[28]

So what is this crushing mountain of debt buying U.S. college students? Well, between the years 2000 and 2007, wages for people with college degrees between the ages of twenty-five and fifty-four dropped 8.5% (and that was *before* the Great Recession).[29]

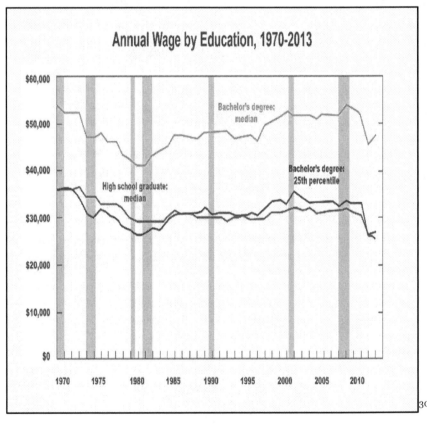

New graduates with Bachelor of Arts degrees are dealing with 8.5% unemployment and a depressing 16.8% underemployment. This means that nearly one out of every ten recent B.A. grads can't find a job at all, and, for those who do, there's nearly a one-in-five chance they'll be stuck in part-time jobs, jobs that have nothing to do with their degree, or jobs that simply don't pay them enough to afford their student debt.

Additionally, despite burying their students in debt, U.S. colleges are still having trouble producing enough Science, Technology, Engineering, and Math graduates to meet the needs of our economy. These S.T.E.M. grads are critical to the global competitiveness of industrialized countries, and U.S. companies import tens of thousands of them from overseas each year.

Combine our college woes with the persistently mediocre global ranking of U.S. students between the ages of six and fifteen (despite the fact that only four countries spend more per student in this age group), and one begins to understand why so many Americans are calling for serious education reforms.[31]

The U.S. isn't the only country dealing with educational crises, either. Even Sweden and the United Kingdom, countries that for years were praised for the quality of their educational systems, have seen their students become far less globally competitive. [32, 33]

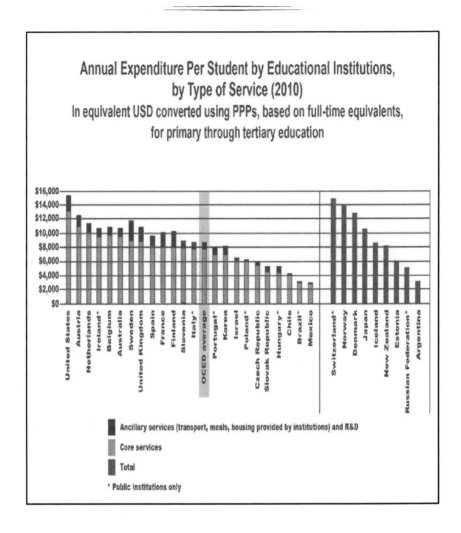

Annual Expenditure Per Student by Educational Institutions, by Type of Service (2010)
In equivalent USD converted using PPPs, based on full-time equivalents, for primary through tertiary education

The Solution

empowr believes that the solution to education's woes can be found when we allow ourselves to view and treat education as a product that, like any other product, will improve dramatically if it's allowed to benefit from the same free-market dynamics that make other products better.

In other words, we need to *make it so the bad teachers can be easily fired.* Second, the *best teachers need to earn as much money—or more—*than most of their best counterparts in industry, making teaching a much more attractive occupation for the best and brightest. Third, *teachers' performances needs to be measured and made transparent* to everyone, especially the product's customers (the students and their parents). And finally, along with access to teacher performance information, students need to *have the power to choose their teachers,* just the same way that we all can choose which car we drive, which mobile phone we buy and which bank we use.

We all saw what happened to the car, telephone, and banking industries—really all industries—in communist countries where consumers had little to no choice: a total disaster. And we also witnessed how those same industries developed in the West, under competitive and free market economics: an explosion of innovation, quality, selection, and value. In exactly the same manner, **education needs to be freed from the centralized control of governments and unions**.

But how do you truly measure a teacher's performance, in order to make the above approach a reality? And how do you free educational systems so as to introduce free-market dynamics?

Fortunately, these are problems that empowr has been working on for many years now, and we'll discuss our solutions in the chapter titled *"empowr's Approach to*

Education." But before we go there, let's take a look at another phenomenon that's quietly having an incredible impact on our lives. To understand what it is, you just need to walk into any classroom today, and you'll notice many students paying far more attention to their smartphone apps than to their teacher. This disturbing phenomenon might actually be the perfect illustration of how education is in decline, while something completely different is taking over our attention and lives. I'm talking about *Network Technology.*

NETWORK TECHNOLOGY SAVED THE WORLD...

As companies and entire industries have gone online, the world has become a much smaller, more efficient place. Tasks that only a couple of decades ago would have taken hours to complete now take a matter of minutes or even seconds. This increased efficiency has made people's lives safer, longer, more productive, and, in many ways, more enjoyable.

In addition to all these positive effects, network technology has allowed information to be shared at nearly unimaginable speeds. This free exchange of information is leading to technological advancements that are drastically improving nearly every aspect of our lives.

There are plenty of people around today who remember a time when international calls were a luxury reserved for special occasions. Back in the mid-20th century, making an international call was a bit of an ordeal. First, you had to leave your nice, warm house and proceed to a telephone office. Once there, you had to grab a card and wait for a phone booth to open up. After that, you had to wait for the operator to connect you to whomever you were calling.

From all accounts, the phone call itself was like shouting into a cave, with your own voice often reverberating back at you from the telephone speaker like a flock of angry bats. The person on the other end of the line was typically so difficult to hear that callers often joked that every long distance phone conversation took place twice in one call, as nearly every sentence had to be repeated at least once.

On top of all this, chances are that the phone company operator was listening in occasionally during the call, so they could disconnect you when the phone call was over. (The grandmother of one of my friends worked as an international switchboard operator, and he says that she has fantastic stories about some of the phone calls she listened to over the years.) Finally, when the call ended, you left your booth and paid a very hefty fee for each minute you'd been on the phone.

Nowadays, there are many different ways to have an international conversation with a friend from the comfort of your couch, using your very own smartphone, tablet, or computer. You can chat with your friend using one of the numerous chat services like Google Talk or Facebook chat, text your buddy instantly using the text feature included on every phone since the 90s, call your friend using your phone's regular dialing feature, or even use Skype, Google Voice, or any of the other freely available VOIP international calling services.

In addition to having your pick of services, you can also have every one of these conversations with little to no call interference and nobody listening in (except for maybe the United States' and/or your own country's National Security Agency). Best of all, many international calls can be made completely free of charge. International calls are just one small example of how network technology has changed an industry. Here are a few more examples that come to mind.

Networked Technologies are Optimizing Humanity

Think back to a time before Google, if you can. Imagine that you needed to find a piece of information. This information could have been an answer to a question about the world or perhaps the name and location of a store that carried a product you needed. Chances are that, to answer the question, you had to consult an encyclopedia or do something really drastic, like ask another human being. To find the store, you might have checked the local phone book.

Now, think about trying to find absolutely any information, product, or service today. Where would you go first? Personally, I'd type whatever it is that I'm looking for into the built-in search box on my internet browser, and Google would probably find exactly what I'm looking for and put it on the very first search page. This process gets more efficient every day since Google's algorithms and access to content are second to none. Consequently, a search that would have taken minutes twenty years ago (or even hours, for harder to answer questions and harder to find products) is now completed in a matter of seconds with a much higher chance of success.

Next, let's think about how you used to buy books (and many other items frequently purchased, nowadays). If your friend told you about a really great book by their favorite author and said that you absolutely had to read it, where would you go to get it? Well, if you were particularly frugal, you might go down to the public library and see if the book was available to check out.

Otherwise, if you wanted to buy the book for yourself, you would have to call the local bookstores to see who had it in stock and then go to purchase it. Alternatively, if, after all this calling around, none of the local book stores had it, you'd have to ask them to order it. This process sometimes took weeks, depending on the popularity of the book. Once the book arrived, they'd call you, and you'd have to drive down to the bookstore to pick it up.

If you want to buy a book today (almost regardless of how hard it is to find), all you need to do is type its name into the search box on Amazon's website, buy the book online, and, if you're an Amazon Prime member (which you should be; it's a great service), you'll probably have it delivered right to your door within a couple of days or be able to download it instantly to a digital device of your choosing (my personal preference). Even if you're not a Prime member, you'll still probably get your book delivered to you in less than a week.

Am I starting to paint a picture for you of how much things have actually changed? Great. Then one more example for good measure won't hurt. I promise it will be an interesting one.

Let's say, twenty years ago, you wanted to have a big party one weekend. Imagine that you hadn't seen a bunch of your friends in a very long time, so you decided to invite all of them to this party and make it a really fancy affair: catering, open bar (because you're classy like that), the whole nine yards. First, you'd have to figure out which of your friends you actually liked enough to invite to your awesome party. You might search through your contact book and find the people you most wanted to see. After that, you'd search the yellow pages for a venue, call around town to find the right caterer, and then put together invitations and mail them out. If you were lucky or really efficient, preparing for your party would probably end up, at the very least, taking a couple of days.

Now, imagine the exact same party today. You invite all your Facebook friends from your "People I Actually Like" list with a few clicks; search Yelp for a caterer; find and reserve the best venue on Google; and the entire process could be over in a matter of minutes. I've already covered Google a bit, but no discussion of how network technology has changed our lives would be complete without touching on the premier social media platform of our time... *Facebook*.

While people like to complain about Facebook, sometimes for valid reasons, nobody can argue that it hasn't revolutionized how people build and maintain their network of friends. It's even redefined the word "friend." (A common question today being, "Is he just your Facebook friend or your real-life friend?") And, despite complaints, a lot folks' lives have been changed for the better because they are a part of Facebook.

In any case, the real point of this last scenario is to show how an activity that, just a few years ago, would have taken a lot of time and energy to complete could possibly take you just minutes to throw together today. Now, multiply all that saved time billions of times over by the many millions of different people who repeatedly use these services, and you start to get an idea of how big an impact network technology has had across the globe.

Finally, look at everything I've written about in this chapter. Twenty years ago, to accomplish all the tasks mentioned, you would have needed an encyclopedia set, a phone book, a clunky old non-portable telephone, transportation to visit physical locations, and a ton of patience. Now, consider how every single thing discussed above can be taken care of from the computer in your home today or on the smartphone in your pocket. And none of these stories even touch on the astonishing benefits that network technology has given to research and development, and has given in support of new technologies across every single profession and field.

To wrap up this chapter, I'll ask you to think about one more thing and then I swear, I'll move on. All the stuff we've talked about so far has pertained primarily to information-oriented tasks, services, and businesses. At the very least, all the physical items being looked for were small and portable. This lack of physical collateral means that a lot of the businesses discussed were either made in the Internet "cloud" or changed fairly easily to leverage the benefits of the cloud.

But, as network technology has evolved, even businesses with significant physical collateral like hotels, taxi services, and airlines (to name just a few) have started to move the majority of their business online to take advantage of the cloud. This trend will someday result in every single product and service that people want being delivered to a physical location of their choosing, based on a request they make from an electronic device they carry with them probably twenty-four hours a day. The future sounds great, right? A utopia where every person gets whatever they want, whenever they want it?

Well, unfortunately, this is the part where I burst everyone's bubble and talk about the *real, imminent, genuinely scary dangers network technology poses* to our world, and the highly quantifiable (and accelerating) destruction it's causing.

THE DARK SIDE OF NETWORK TECHNOLOGY

The free exchange of information that network technology has brought about has also led to a winner-take-all marketplace where the first business to effectively leverage the cloud by going online and taking advantage of "The Network Effect" ends up dominating each field. This has already created huge, shockingly powerful monopolies that stifle competition and innovation in addition to reduce the number of jobs available in a given field.

In the future, as more businesses become fully networked, it is likely that each major category of business will end up utterly controlled by one monstrously influential global corporation. This in turn will concentrate obscene wealth and political power in the hands of a small, elite group, while leaving huge swaths of humanity unemployed and disenfranchised. Unless...

F ive months.
That's all it took to block an industry giant from gaining control of the entire Japanese market.

Yahoo had lusted after the Japanese auction market for a long time, while planning its strategy of attack. Despite a great deal of skepticism on whether the Japanese would even be interested in online auctions, Yahoo assigned four of their best people to develop the site. At the same time, the leading force in the online auction industry, eBay, was also plotting its entry into the Japanese market. As the development teams in each company worked at a feverish pace, everybody knew that the first player on the scene would have a distinct advantage.

In September 1999, Yahoo Japan launched its auction site, beating eBay to the market by only five months. This advantage, combined with marketing tactics that skillfully targeted new Japanese users, resulted in Yahoo Japan's essentially completely shutting eBay out of the Japanese market and laying claim to the tens of millions of dollars in revenue that the market produced each year. When the CEO of Yahoo Japan, Masahiro Inoue, was asked why being first to the market was so critical, he answered, "We knew catching up with a front-runner is hard because, in auctions, more buyers bring more sellers."[34]

The principal that Mr. Inoue stated above, often referred to as the "first-mover advantage," is one that applies far beyond the online auction market. Being the first to successfully enter a market has always been important to business. But with the introduction of network technology, the importance of being the "first mover" has been elevated to existential levels for businesses.

This is to a large degree a result of the fact that Mr. Inoue states very clearly: *more buyers bring more sellers* who, in turn, attract more buyers, creating an upward-accelerating phenomenon that means, within only a few months, competitors to that first-mover platform find it nearly impossible to enter the market or survive. Whether discussing online auctions or any other online business, the principle remains the same.

Network technology amplifies the first-mover advantage through something called "The Network Effect." I can feel readers' eyes glossing over as I type this, so let me assure you up front that I'm going to keep this explanation as short and sweet as possible.

The Network Effect (also called the Law of Telecosm) essentially states that ***as more "nodes" (or users) connect to a network, the value of the network (to its customers, shareholders, and other stakeholders) goes up exponentially*** as opposed to linearly:

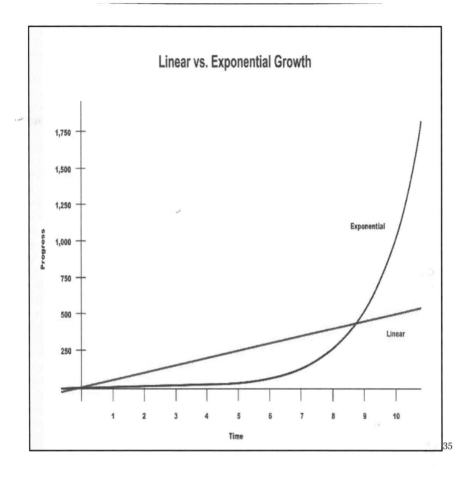

Think of it like this: If, at one point, you owned the only telephone in the world, it would be pretty much useless because there would be nobody else to talk to. But when somebody else gets a telephone, all of a sudden your phone is worth a whole hell of a lot more, because now you have somebody to talk to (other than yourself). As more people and businesses get phones, the value of having a phone goes up, as does the value of the entire telephone network. Eventually, everybody wants and needs a telephone, because there are so many people and businesses to talk to. Like with any type of network, as each new person connects to the network, the value provided by the network goes up exponentially, not linearly.

I'll give one more quick example, just to make sure you understand. If you already get it (or just plain don't care), feel free to skip it.

Way back in the days when the operating system field wasn't completely dominated by the kingdoms of Microsoft and Apple, International Business Machines (IBM) was contending with Microsoft in the personal computer operating system market. Having once been partners on the development of a new operating system called OS/2, the competition between the two companies was particularly fierce. While Microsoft and its operating system, Windows, enjoyed a number of advantages over IBM and OS/2, two key factors led primarily to Microsoft ultimately winning the war:

1. Microsoft got Windows preloaded on many thousands of personal computers. This put Windows at a distinct advantage over IBM's OS/2, which had to be purchased separately.
2. Because of that, many more software developers began to create programs for Microsoft's Windows operating system. This meant that users who had Windows gained access to a much greater variety of programs.

If you look at the two factors individually, they each appear important but not necessarily critical. However, if you put them together, you see how powerful a combination they make: Developers wanted their programs to be bought by as many consumers as possible, and since computers were coming preloaded with Windows, it made more sense for developers to design their programs for Windows machines.

And consumers wanted to be able to use as many programs as possible, so it made sense for them to choose Windows because it had more programs built for it.

The operating system with more programs (Windows) attracted more consumers; and the one with more consumers (Windows) attracted more developers and programs.

Fast forward a couple of decades, through many repeats of this cycle, and now almost nobody knows what OS/2 is or was, but nearly everybody who has ever used a computer knows about Microsoft Windows.

Now, let's move on to why network technology poses such a frightening long-term threat to humanity.

As more and more companies in every imaginable industry hook up to the Internet and their business models continue to take more advantage of network technologies, the Network Effect becomes a bigger factor in their industry.

At first, when a business begins to experience the Network Effect, it sees increased growth in the value it can provide to customers. This draws more and more customers to the business which, of course, increases revenues. As revenues go through the roof and the business is able to control an increasingly larger share of its market, smart investors in the industry start to see the writing on the wall and begin to divest from its competitors, investing exclusively in the inevitable champion of the winner-takes-all game that's been set in motion. The value of the networked company continues to increase by leaps and bounds, giving it even more resources, which enable it to provide even more value to customers and take over an even greater share of customers, profits, investors, suppliers and other limited industry resources.

As the business that first leverages the Network Effect takes off into the stratosphere, its competitors soon become unable to raise money because nobody wants to buy their stock. Even worse, it gets harder for competitors to acquire new customers because they can't provide anywhere near the same value that the fully networked business is able to give. The competitors' stock prices plummet, they are forced to lay off many employees, and, eventually, each competitor goes out of business, turning the most networked company into a monopoly.

Without competitive pressures pushing them to innovate, monopolies stop progressing. Their products and services remain the same for longer and longer periods. To make their shareholders happy, they easily generate higher and higher profits by incrementally increasing the prices of their stale products and services, which they can easily do because customers have nowhere else to go. Slowly but surely, the entire category of business they dominate stagnates.

While consumers often benefit from the incredible value monopolies *initially* provide, in the end almost everybody suffers from monopolization. Society misses out on all the product selection, quality, and value that would have existed in a more competitive arena.

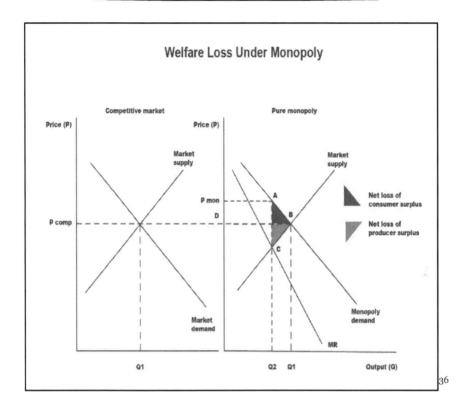

Even more importantly, the gradual disappearance of competitors and their associated partners, vendors, and supporting ecosystem means fewer people are required to operate the less robust industry.

Going forward, as all companies continue their rush toward adopting network technologies in order to exploit the Network Effect and win their industry's coveted monopoly position (before their competitors do), one industry category after another will become dominated by Goliath monopolies, creating more unemployment and underemployment (where people are forced to take low-paying jobs they don't want).

The Scariest Category of All

One specific industry category that's creating more unemployment and misery is that of the *pure web tech giants.* They are taking greatest advantage of the Network Effect because they are nothing if not giant networks. These are the web and social media companies that we're all quite familiar with: Facebook, Twitter, Tumblr, Instagram, and Pinterest, to name just a few. Google falls under that category, too, because its primary business model is simply a network scheme that brings together businesses looking for customers with customers searching for the things those businesses offer.

As these web models first evolved, consumers, in their haste to take advantage of the services these companies offer, basically failed to say, "Hey, wait a minute. Your *entire* business model depends on the relationships, communications, and/or searching activity of me and others like me... So where's my share?" The result is what I like to call the Great Disappearing Act—in that, massive amounts of society's productivity, progress, innovation, and value are being exchanged for something worth much less.

For those of you who like numbers, let's take a look at what's been happening in America, as an example:

The United States, as a nation, spends the equivalent of twelve million work years (a work year is 52 forty-hour work weeks per year) on social media annually, the equivalent of over $300 billion dollars at the average U.S. person's salary level of $24,000.[37] So, Americans are giving up $300 billion dollars' worth of their time and receiving virtually nothing of monetary value in exchange. Facebook, the social network that receives most of that time, generated $1.83 billion from its U.S. users in the fourth quarter of 2014.[38] That means that, in America alone, each year we're exchanging the majority of $300 billion worth of our time for about $7 billion in revenues *for Facebook*—a disappearing act of 97% for society as a whole.

Extractive vs. Inclusive Economics

One of the many geniuses that has advised empowr, M.I.T.'s professor of economics and one of the ten most cited economists in the world, Daron Acemoglu [39] , wrote a bestselling book titled *Why Nations Fail*, in which he discusses how most countries were originally set up to *extract* as much money from their economies as possible for the benefit of a few elite people at the top, leading those nations to fail economically. That's called **extractive economics.**

On the other hand, the nations that succeed economically are the ones that figure out how to be **inclusive,** meaning their policies and institutions are organized in a way to ensure that any value taken *out* of economies, such as taxes, are intelligently put back *into* the economy in ways that help further grow their economies and help their people improve their lives.

Many nations, such as Argentina, Peru and Mexico, were originally built by settlers who arrived from more developed countries with a goal of *extracting* as much value as possible from these new lands, and who turned the locals into slaves, using force to extract natural resources and send those resources back to the kingdoms that financed their missions.

Those extractive approaches to economics resulted in widespread misery, economic failure, and cultural norms that, in many cases, still continue to this day.

In many ways, this is what is happening on the web today. In other words, Facebook's $7 billion in annual revenues (generated from its U.S. territory) and associated profits—generated from nearly $300 billions' worth of American's time—ends up going to a tiny number of Facebook's major shareholders and a small number employees (relative to its user base; only 7,200 employees as of early 2015[40]). This is exactly the definition of extractive economics, and, as those numbers clearly illustrate, it's having a damaging effect on the economy of the United States as well as every country in which Facebook operates. And it's something that must change, or the world will end up in a very bad place soon, as we'll discuss in the next chapter. (Addressing this problem was a primary reason that empowr was created. Details on exactly how empowr will help, in the chapter titled *"Strategically Leveraging the Network Effect."*

"Now, hold on," some of you will say. "Society benefits from the services that Facebook, Google, and other networks offer to their users for free."

I agree. But I argue that the economic value of the services offered by these companies for free to their users, pales in relative economic value to that which society loses in the process, as measured, for example, by the $300 billion of worker time that disappeared in the marketplace. In addition, there are no taxes collected on free services; therefore, funding for schools, roads, and other government services disappeared along with all that economic value.

Today's social networks rate very low in Overall Labor Effectiveness (OLE), a key performance indicator that measures the utilization, performance, and quality of any workforce and its impact on productivity.

If the economic model of current social networks worked well from a macroeconomic perspective, each dollar's worth of worker time consumed by the network would translate into something greater than one dollar in economic output. And, of course, that output could be taxed, bringing back more to society as a whole.

The good news is that capitalism is great at motivating people to figure out what the best uses of scarce resources are. And that's why it's only a matter of time until someone presents a better model than Facebook's, which sets the bar quite low since it takes each dollar's worth of labor and shrinks it into a mere three pennies.

At empowr, we've taken another approach, and that's to first carefully study history to discover what happened over centuries within countries, which are the original large social networks, of course.

What we learned from our research and then spent the next fifteen years attempting to implement is the idea of offering an *inclusive* alternative to users. When America declared its independence and later collected taxes from citizens, those revenues belonged to its citizens, not to a small number of kings, lords, and knights (as was the case in Great Britain, for example). In other words, tax revenues were spent to build roads and bridges, educate citizens, and protect them—all things that helped average everyday citizens to increase their economic output. The result of this *inclusive* approach (as opposed to an *extractive* approach) was that America's share of global GDP shot up more than thirty-fold—from a fraction of 1% to nearly 30%—in just over a single century:

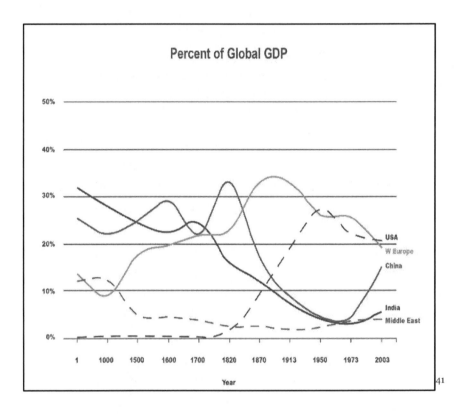

Finally, some of you will argue that what people are doing on Facebook should not be viewed as work; rather it's all just communication—or even entertainment, just like watching TV or listening to the radio.

But is there really any question about whether watching TV for hours each day is good (or ended up being good) for individuals or society as a whole? There's a very simple but strong correlation that can be drawn between when TV started to take up hours of people's time each day, and when society started getting dumber, less knowledgeable, and less productive, but let's not go there right now.

Instead, close your eyes and imagine for a moment that with the help of some new technology, we could turn that very same communication and entertainment into actual economically productive activities—converting each dollar worth of time spent in the platform into something greater than a dollar in economic output—creating opportunity for individuals and progress for society. If that could be accomplished without any loss of communication or entertainment value, would you consider it an important advancement?

Building the World's First Inclusive Online Economy

If corporations can figure out how to be inclusive as opposed to extractive, not only will their customers love them like never before (resulting in more loyal customers who spend more money with them per customer), but they'll also end up making more profits for their shareholders in the long run—much in the same way that the United States now boasts the largest number of billionaires in the world, and why the U.S. government is the most powerful and wealthiest organization in the world, even though it spends all the tax money it collects on serving its citizens.

Being inclusive as a corporation is much harder than it sounds. First, company shareholders have to be convinced that giving back profits to customers is a sound business decision (for them). empowr decided early on to *not* bring in investors. Yes, that resulted in varying levels of poverty and misery for about 1,000 employees who (because they believed in empowr's mission) left high paying jobs to work for little or no pay for some or all of the fifteen years it took to develop the empowr platform. As a result of their sacrifices, empowr is now in the incredibly unique position to adopt an inclusive approach to its economics and distribute its profits to its customers, because it has no Wall Street shareholders or venture capitalists to convince.

Without a doubt, other companies that want to take the same inclusive approach will have a much harder time convincing their stakeholders (shareholders, investors, and board members) to go along. The upshot is that, by being the first to do this, empowr hopes to provide a real live example that other companies can show their investors when they, too, set out to win the argument that inclusive approaches will not only attract more loyal customers and revenues but will ultimately lead to higher profits for shareholders in the long run—in the same way that inclusive countries *ultimately* created more wealth for everyone involved, including normal citizens *AND* wealthy stakeholders.

In addition to the hurdles presented by company shareholders, giving back profits to customers requires many new inventions and technologies that can accomplish everything from effectively distributing money to customers, to blocking fraudsters looking to take advantage of those distributions. Luckily, empowr has spent the last fifteen years building virtually all of the required technologies, techniques and know-how, and **we intend to *give* all of these to companies of all types, sizes and industries.** We'll discuss this later in this book.

To be clear, Facebook and Google are hardly alone out there as pure network plays that are effectively killing the economy. Skype (with only 500 employees; 2010) is putting massive phone companies (and their employees) out in the cold, as is Automattic/WordPress (322 employees), WhatsApp (55 employees), Mozilla (1,000 employees), Tumblr (271), Twitter (3900 around the world), Opera Software (1,029), Canonical (500 in 30+ countries), Wikimedia/Wikipedia (250), and Craigslist—which has almost single-handedly put newspapers out of business—has a mere 40-some employees in San Francisco.

In the grand scheme of things, the Internet's Network Effect is just getting started but is already causing mass unemployment, and that's on top of unemployment caused by automation coming in to replace workers, such as the ways that software and search engines are replacing travel agents, phone operators, video-rental and record store employees.

Or look at what happened in Detroit, Michigan, where assembly line robots and other forms of automation replaced autoworkers in the car, truck, and automotive parts plants once thriving in the 1950s and '60s.[42]

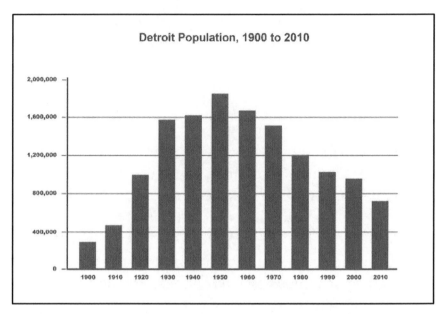

Eric Byrnjolfsson, another well-respected American author and academic from M.I.T., described in his book, *Race Against the Machine*, an exchange between Ford CEO Henry Ford II and United Automobile Workers president Walter Reuther, as they toured a heavily automated automobile factory.

> *"Ford jokingly jabs at Reuther: "Walter, how are you going to get these robots to pay UAW dues?" Not missing a beat, Reuther responds: "Henry, how are you going to get them to buy your cars?"*

The result of all of this is that society's jobs (that people actually want) are disappearing en masse on the one hand, while, on the other hand, a huge amount of wealth is moving to the tiny, elite parts of society comprised of either owners or essential and highly skilled employees of category-killing monopolies—leading to mass *technological unemployment.*

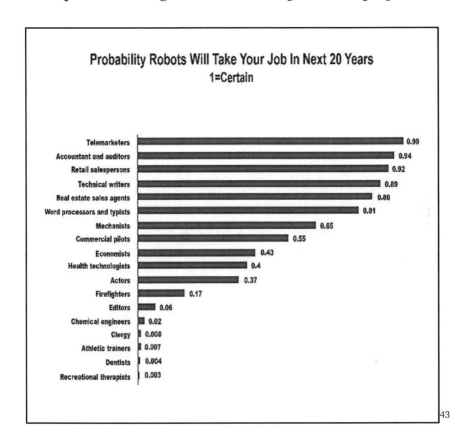

In the Coming Years Nearly Every Major Industry Will Become Very Highly Networked and/or Automated

To get an idea of the effect that automation and the Network Effect have already had on your life and on the world, let's play a little game. Bear with me: I promise I won't take too long to get to the point.

Think of the last time you bought any type of music. Chances are that many of you either haven't bought music in a very long time or, if you did, it was purchased or rented through one of the giant online music platforms such as Spotify, Pandora, or iTunes.

Next, try and remember when you last purchased a book and where you purchased it. While there are still plenty of places to purchase books, for the time being, the dominant force in the industry, Amazon, is growing larger and more monopolistic every year.

How about the last time you searched for information? As discussed elsewhere in this book, you probably didn't grab a dictionary or a sports almanac. You almost certainly didn't go to your favorite shelf full of encyclopedias or head to your local library. I would bet good money that you probably "Googled" it.

Or think of the last time you watched a movie or a show on anything other than a television. It was likely Netflix, Amazon, or Hulu. You may have even been extra sneaky and watched your movie or show on one of the *many* illegal sites that new technology has given the ability to broadcast pirated videos across the globe mere hours after they air.

The upshot of all of this is that, in every single scenario above, thousands upon thousands of jobs are being made either obsolete or much less important each year, as technology does more of the work in each industry. With each of the business models above, musicians, writers, website creators, telephone operators, truck drivers, movie creators, and the other everyday people who work in each of those industries receive a smaller share of the profits as time goes by.

As all services eventually become more and more digitized, the owners of the networks (and the servers that run the algorithms) end up with a frightening level of control over their particular industries. And every week, they quietly tweak their algorithms to ensure that, gradually, the vast majority of the revenue their industry produces goes right into their pockets.

We won't have to wait long to see the next generation of technological unemployment. A report from the University of Oxford recently predicted over a 90% chance that fast food workers will be replaced by machines in relatively short order.[44] Another example is that, thanks in large part to websites like Travelocity, Orbitz, and Expedia, over 38,000 travel agent jobs have disappeared since 2002.[45]

Even soldiers and police officers may someday soon have their jobs taken over by machines.[46] Professionals aren't safe from being automated into obsolescence or irrelevance, either. Legendary tech venture capitalist Vinod Khosla (someone who was early to understand some of empowr's promise and goals, as evidenced by his repeated aggressive attempts to buy a piece of empowr) predicts that, in short order, 80% of what doctors currently do will be replaced by robots.[47]

And those are just a few examples. Because of growing technological unemployment and the rapid monopolization of entire industries due to the Network Effect along with deteriorating educational systems and dysfunctional governments, the world is facing some huge challenges and will, undoubtedly, face even bigger challenges in the near future. So, to be perfectly honest, as it stands now, things look pretty grim.

Even "grim" might be a bit too sugar-coated, so I'll just call it like I see it, instead.

THE WORLD'S EXPERIENCING PROBLEMS THAT THREATEN HUMANITY'S FUTURE

Yet, as a result of setbacks with democracy, education, and technology, many countries are being governed very ineffectively, and voters are either too uneducated or too worried about providing for their families to do anything about it. This is making it much harder for the world community to effectuate the changes that are needed to avoid catastrophe.

Between climate change, terrorism, technological unemployment, pandemics, economic collapses, natural disasters, and growing first-world inequality, there are some very serious issues facing our species that require equally serious solutions.

So, to summarize the bad news covered in the first half of this book:

> ➢ First-world democracies are being hijacked by special interests and big money;
> ➢ Educational systems are leaving students woefully unprepared to participate in the modern, global economy where only highly skilled labor jobs matter, as software and automation replace low skill jobs;
> ➢ Network technologies are making it much easier for single corporations to rapidly take over entire industries and form job destroying monopolies;
> ➢ To add insult to injury, each structural problem is making the others even worse, leaving the human race completely unequipped to face the many complex threats facing humanity.

I understand if you winced a little while reading all that; it wasn't particularly fun writing it, either. That said, in the interest of clarity, I'd like to elaborate just a little on these points before moving forward to examine what we believe are the most dangerous global problems. I promise I'll make it fast.

First, the hijacking of democracy has left the *governments of many influential countries unable or unwilling to respond to the worldwide issues humanity must deal with*. As a species, we're facing challenges that very clearly require visionary leadership and innovative thinking to address them comprehensively.

At the same time, because of the erosion of democracy in leading countries such as the United States, the governments that would be most able to push forward international efforts to meet these global challenges are being held back by utterly dysfunctional political systems. As the world watches this dysfunction unfold, global enthusiasm for democracy wanes, and other more dangerous forms of government (which we'll discuss later) become more appealing. This puts humanity in danger of backsliding.

48 49

Meanwhile, many educational systems are failing to give students the skills they need to succeed in the post-industrial workforce and become productive members of society.

Even as secondary and postsecondary education becomes more important to prosperity, underfunded schools are forced to hire teachers from the bottom half of graduating classes. Those teachers go on to inadequately educate their students, many of whom eventually go on to become the next generation of teachers. As this happens, a "dumbification cycle" is created which produces consistently less capable graduates each time the cycle repeats. Consequently, students around the world are expressing their frustration with schools they see as having wasted years of their life, actually sabotaging their chances of success rather than enhancing them.

Next, while democracy and education falter, the Network Effect threatens to create behemoth global corporations that monopolize entire fields. As these tech-heavy companies evolve, they shed their human assets in favor of more efficient robotic workers. This leads to unemployment, which shrinks the middle class, concentrating wealth and political power at the top to an even greater degree.

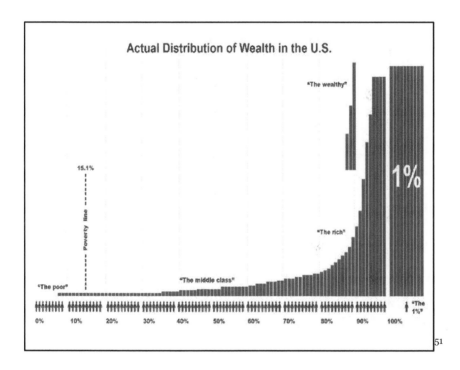

These social, political, and economic structural problems are putting many of the world's most powerful countries in a position where they aren't equipped to deal with important crises, e.g., climate change, government shutdowns, the expansion of international terror networks, and the global spread of drug resistant diseases, to name but a few.

There are other examples:

- ✓ We are still exploring new fossil fuel resources even though our top scientists tell us that our burning of the many fossil fuels we have already extracted will cause irreversible global catastrophe.
- ✓ Major political parties across the world are becoming more polarized each year, as each election cycle pushes them further away from the center.
- ✓ Rather than find ways to properly integrate disaffected segments of society, many countries are choosing to go down dangerous, authoritarian paths in order to feel secure against global terror.
- ✓ Despite their role in creating superbugs, antibiotics are still one of the most over-prescribed medications in the world, leading to more resilient and deadly diseases every year.

And, while all the problems discussed in this chapter are real and require serious attention, there are **three core problems** that worry us, at empowr, the most (and for which we've spent the last decade and a half working on solutions):

- ➢ Poverty and inequality
- ➢ Terrorism and extremism; and
- ➢ The backsliding and destruction of democracy.

THE GROWING DANGERS OF POVERTY AND INEQUALITY

At first glance, statistics show that poverty and inequality may be problems that are shrinking at a rapid rate. However, in large part because of China's unsustainable economic growth, assessing either statistic on a global level is misleading.

The fact is that inequality in industrialized nations grows worse every year, and, when China is excluded from measures of global poverty, the problem seems barely to have been addressed by some of the world's poorest regions.

This should concern everybody because both issues, historically, have had some very nasty consequences.

In recent years, leaders around the world have been patting themselves on the back over the perceived progress in the global fight against poverty. And, to their credit, a few aspects of worldwide poverty are being addressed in some noteworthy ways: for example, the global childhood mortality rate has fallen by nearly 50% since 1990; pregnant women in many poorer countries are receiving improved prenatal care. On the surface, even the overarching problem of global poverty itself *appears* to have been addressed meaningfully in the past two decades, with the poverty rate falling 25%-30% since 1981.

Unfortunately, a more detailed examination of the poverty numbers shows that China accounts for the *vast* majority of the reduction in global poverty. This is largely due to the *huge* trade surplus China has been running for the past decade, with industrialized nations pumping *tens of billions* of dollars into its economy every year.

Without China, improvements in global poverty have been mediocre at best, with only a dismal 5%-10% reduction over the course of the past two decades contrasted with huge advancements in technology and the continued march of globalization. Adding insult to injury, in a number of critical regions, the number of people living in poverty has actually *increased* in recent years, with sub-Saharan Africa being among the most worrisome.[52]

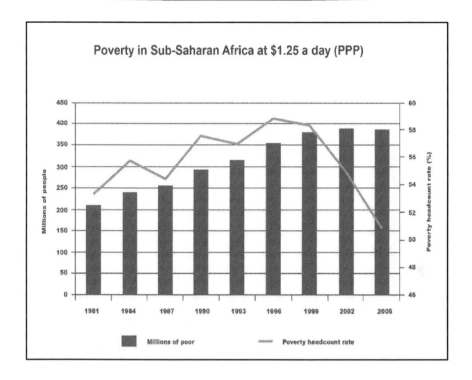

Worse, as I'll discuss in greater detail later on, China's current economic model is simply not sustainable in the long term.[53] The impact that the shrinking of China's trade surplus will have within its own borders and on the global poverty numbers is not certain. But, as democratic reforms are slowly rolled back within that country, as income inequality grows (now even exceeding U.S. numbers), as a monstrous real estate bubble prepares to burst, and as some minority populations become further disenfranchised every year, many global authorities have begun to express a great deal of concern.[54]

Inequality is a Growing Problem for the World's Most Powerful and Influential Nations

Even though inequality has been "reduced" on a global level, rising rates of inequality in the world's most powerful countries threaten everything from the effectiveness and desirability of democracy to the very stability of the global economy. Worldwide inequality has fallen as wealth from industrialized nations and their post-industrial economies has been pumped into developing countries, due in large part to the availability of cheap manufacturing labor within those countries. Despite this phenomenon, many first-world nations are being forced to come to terms with the issues created by increased economic inequality within their own borders.

The United States is perhaps the best example of the threat posed by this growing first-world inequality. The percentage of national wealth controlled by the top 1% of American society has skyrocketed since 1980. While the share of U.S. income going to the top 1% of earners has jumped over the past half century, America's middle-class has seen its income growth stagnate, and some of the poorest segments of society have seen their standards of living actually fall. Currently, over 45 million Americans and nearly one out of every five American children live in poverty.[55] [56]

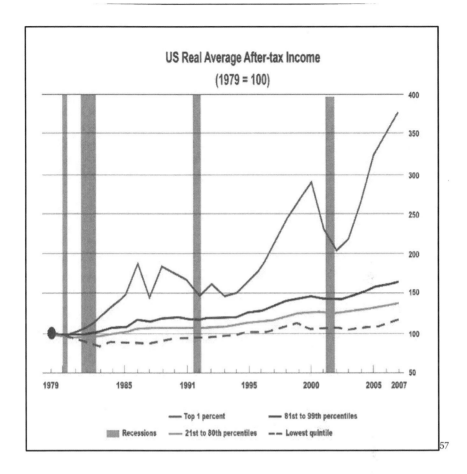

US Real Average After-tax Income
(1979 = 100)

This doesn't just pose an *enormous* credibility and public relations problem for a country that has been selling the American Dream to the world for the past century. As inequality grows, so do a number of very severe problems, such as declining social mobility, decreased political stability, a less healthy population, reduced child well-being, increased prevalence of mental illness, rising prison populations, and lower educational scores, to name just a few.[58] The damage that inequality is causing to the very fabric of society in a number of industrialized nations comes as no surprise to many historians and prominent public figures who, for years, have been warning of the dangers that inequality poses to our world.[59]

The upshot of these two growing problems is that the gains that have been made in first-world nations since the end of World War II are being threatened by the very issues they committed to addressing in other developing and third-world nations back in the 1990s. The irony of this situation could be humorous, if not for the fact that poverty and inequality have led to revolutions or even worse, over the course of human history.

INEQUALITY AND POVERTY CREATE TERRIBLE GOVERNMENTS

Historically, poverty and inequality have driven many countries into the hands of dictators and other very bad people. As people get so poor that they have little (or nothing) to lose, the appeal of charismatic leaders who promise better times starts to increase, regardless of the ideology those leaders espouse.

As a result, poverty and inequality have been the key causes behind many of history's most violent revolutions and international conflicts.

The economic collapse came swiftly and without warning. It seemed as if, almost overnight, the town's bustling streets had been deserted. Where once you could find a merchant or a performer on every corner, suddenly there were just beggars or transients. As the wealth quickly drained from the city, areas of town that were once frequented by families took on a new, dangerous character. Only the bravest or most foolhardy residents willingly visited these new ghettos, and those who did made a point to keep their wits about them and their hands on their valuables, some even going so far as to arm themselves in a place where such precautions would have been cause for laughter only a year before.

The few businesses that managed to still stay open put bars over their windows to prevent vandals and robbers from breaking in during the dead of night and destroying or stealing what little was left. These ugly coal-black metal bars seemed to match perfectly the feeling of despair that clung to all other surfaces. While many of the remaining businesses tried to keep their prices as low as they could, often taking losses on their few sales, even the cheapest merchandise became less affordable for the city's residents with each passing day. The owners of the handful of shops and booths still left open watched with hope as each rare pedestrian approached, only to hang their heads in all-too-familiar disappointment as each person inevitably passed them by.

Meanwhile, just outside the city limits, factories that had once employed thousands of citizens in jobs that allowed workers to provide for themselves and their families, stood idle, staffed only by a few local pigeons or the occasional migratory bird passing through on its journey to a faraway destination. The ports and docks that in better times had imported goods from distant lands were now occupied by only a few barnacled fishing boats.

The entire country seemed to be shriveling on the vine, as children went to bed hungry and previously happy couples fought tooth and nail over the smallest trivialities. Those unfortunate enough to be struck with serious illness either withered away in dark corners or took to the streets, hoping that somebody, anybody, would help them. Everywhere the air hung heavy with anger, frustration, and the raw desperation of broken humanity.

But, there was still hope to be found if one looked hard enough...

A man, decrying the old ways and talking about new, revolutionary ideas, was gaining a following. He knew who was to blame for the current destitute state of affairs. He'd seen how the others lived, in their giant houses with pets that ate better than most people. The stories of how the rich laughed at the regular folks and thought of them as less than human were difficult to believe, but how else could one explain how little they did to help the poor, sick, and starving?

As more and more people flocked to his banner, the man gained in power. No longer were his words shrugged off by those in control as just another petty annoyance. They began to fear him and his new ideas. They saw the new world he was trying to build, and it terrified them. Some of the few powerful factions not already marching to the man's new tune tried to fight him, to hold back the rising tide, but it was already too late. The battles were bloody and vicious, but their outcome was never really in question.

The people had finally found hope, and no matter what it cost them or their country, they were going to chase that hope wherever it led them.

Learning From The Past

The story I've just told you has played out a thousand or more times over the course of human history, in one form or another. Sure, a number of details change, depending on which revolution or political collapse is being discussed, but, at the core of each scenario you found people who had grown tired of being unable to feed themselves or their children. As the famous Greek philosopher Aristotle once said, "Poverty is the parent of revolution and crime."

I'll give you a few examples from history. I'm sure you will recognize most of them.

A famously bad German painter was once in the position that only a few hundred people believed anything he said was worth listening to. The German people at the time were doing quite well, despite the onerous sanctions imposed on them by the victors of World War I, through the Treaty of Versailles.

Sure, their economy was dependent upon exporting manufactured goods to other countries, but, because the factories and businesses that made those goods were able to pay their workers a living wage, Germans had very little interest in a man with a strange mustache and a dime store philosophy filled with far too much hate and not nearly enough intelligence. They could feed their children, pay their rent, and even afford to take vacations to one of the many beautiful places in their country, so why put any stock in the rantings of a deluded madman?

But, after the Great Depression hit the United States and the unprecedented global recession it caused spread to Germany, things changed very quickly. All of a sudden, the madman's arguments started to make more sense, and the hate that he spewed found a home in the hearts of Germans who felt betrayed by not only their countrymen, but by the entire world. Eventually, that madman (who you might have already guessed was Adolph Hitler) rose to power in large part because of the German peoples' poverty. He went on to cause the most destructive war that our planet has ever seen and manipulated his countrymen into committing some of the worst atrocities in the history of humanity.

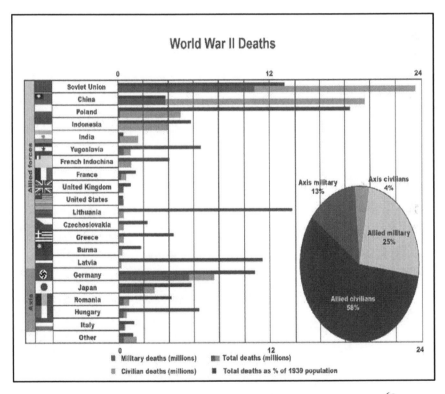

"World War II Casualties" Wikimedia Commons[60]

Hitler's story isn't entirely unlike that of a young man who grew up is Russia's Caucasus Mountains. Russian society at the time was dominated by a few elite groups and ruled with an iron fist by the Czars. These groups owned the vast majority of the farmland and nearly all the factories. The Russian peasants were paid poverty-level wages to toil away in factories and on farms, often for fourteen hours a day and typically without any weekend break. The rents most peasants paid for their land were outrageous, often forcing people who cultivated acres of land to go hungry just to afford to stay on their farms. On top of all this, for those stupid, angry, or hopeless enough to get out of line, floggings were a traditional form of punishment.

The poverty and inequality that pervaded Russian society led to a thriving Bolshevik movement which espoused the beliefs of the founder of Communism, Karl Marx. The young man I mentioned earlier was a part of this movement. Communist ideology offered the millions of Russians living in poverty some hope that, when assets and wealth were redistributed, their lives would improve. Many Russians' lives were so terrible already that plenty of them thought they had very little to lose. Eventually, the Bolsheviks incited a rebellion that allowed them to take control over the entire country.

The story is complicated (as Russian stories often are), but the long and short of it is that the young man, Joseph Stalin, rose to power on the coattails of another famous man named Vladimir Lenin, who controlled the Bolshevik Communist movement. Once Lenin fell ill as the result of an assassination attempt, Stalin quickly rose to be the unquestioned leader of Russia, which was eventually called the Soviet Union.

The Soviet Union's prison camps (known as gulags) and secret police force (KGB) are famous to this day for their brutality and for the hundreds of thousands of Russian lives they destroyed. Stalin, after playing a critical role in the defeat of Hitler (his one-time ally) during World War II, put the Soviet Union at odds with the United States. This ultimately led to the Cold War, which resulted in the economic collapse of the Soviet Union and forced the U.S.'s national debt to skyrocket over the course of the conflict. The Cold War also took the world to the very brink of thermonuclear annihilation.

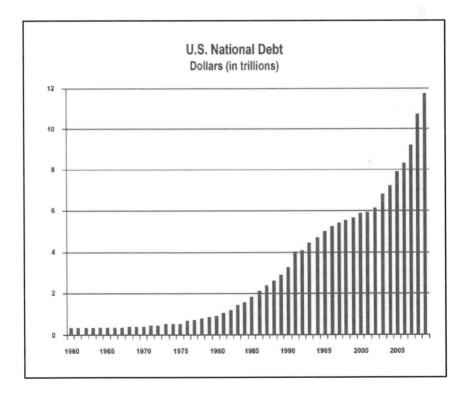

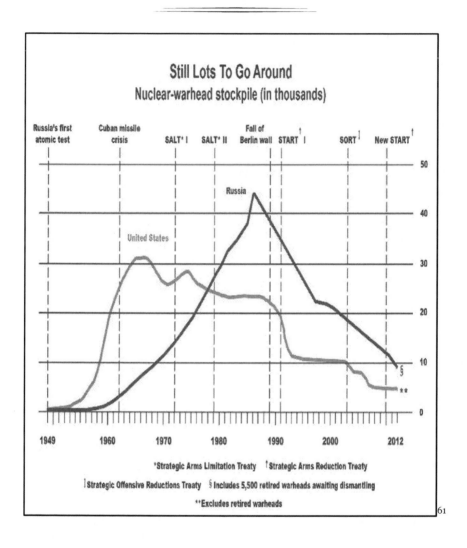

Still Lots To Go Around
Nuclear-warhead stockpile (in thousands)

*Strategic Arms Limitation Treaty   †Strategic Arms Reduction Treaty

‡Strategic Offensive Reductions Treaty   §Includes 5,500 retired warheads awaiting dismantling

**Excludes retired warheads

History tends to move in cycles, which is why there's an expression that those who don't learn from history are doomed to repeat it. If you think of the rise of dictators as a brutal, tragic game, the playbook that aspiring dictators use is tried and true. Poverty and inequality are the arenas in which the game is played, and they facilitate its every step forward.

The Dictator Playbook

While there are often many nuances and subtleties to the game, its basic progression almost always follows five basic steps.

Step One: *Poverty and inequality create an undemocratic state* in which the bottom segments of a society don't control enough wealth to provide for themselves, and they wield little to no political power so they cannot hope to affect any structural changes to the system they live under. This situation creates enough desperation and anger among everyday people that they become much more vulnerable to the lure of any political system other than the one that's making their lives so miserable.

Step Two: *A new, often charismatic leader* connects with the poor and disenfranchised masses, convincing them that he truly feels their pain. Sometimes, this may even be true, as a number of dictators have started out from the lower classes, themselves. In any case, after the new leader convinces enough people that he understands how they feel, he gives them *a target for their hate*. Another group of people, another country, an ideology—it doesn't really matter what it is, just so long as he can make an even mildly convincing argument that the target is the cause of most of the society's ills.

Step Three: *The leader takes power*. This could be through an election or through some kind of revolution. The method of how our soon-to-be dictator rises to power isn't as important as what he does once he gets there.

Step Four: Once in power, our budding dictator starts *squashing all dissenting voices* both outside of his own organization and within it. Think media censorship, purges, and the government takeover of all forms of mass communication.

Source: Reporters Without Borders: For Freedom of Information[62]

Step Five: Once the fourth step is complete, our newly minted *dictator extraordinaire ensures that there are no term limits that interfere with him ruling for long periods of* time or he takes steps to cement his power to the point where any "elections" that do take place are complete farces. (North Korea is an example of the latter.) After a person or group of people reach the top of a government and make it so that almost no matter what happens, they will never have to worry about being removed from power, any hope of democratic or representative government dies a quick death.

You'll remember in an earlier chapter when we talked about the fat, lazy company that can't compete without having a monopoly because of how stagnant and inefficient it becomes. Well, that company parallels quite effectively the makeup and evolution of totalitarian regimes. As the people at the top consolidate their power further and further with each passing year, they get lazier and more reliant on their traditional way of doing things.

One difference is that, if they are ruthless enough, they can maintain a monopoly on governance that lasts for decades, no matter how badly they run things or how poor they make the majority of the people they "govern." Eventually, poverty and inequality in dictator-run countries do tend to become bad enough that there's another, often bloodier, revolution and the process begins all over again.

This self-perpetuating cycle of poverty and non-democracy, which my team and I call "the Poverty Loop," is one of the primary reasons we created empowr. Later in this book we'll get into the nitty-gritty of how empowr is designed to short circuit the Poverty Loop by attacking poverty head on, but, for the time being, suffice it to say that we believe if we can help nip poverty and inequality in the bud—while also delivering a functional democracy via the Internet—we can play at least a small role in preventing *a lot of pretty awful stuff* from happening across the world.

Throughout history, nearly every single time that any government appears where the leaders are not regularly replaced through nonviolent means, corruption starts to grow, and *bad things happen.* There are even world leaders today who have risen to power based on the poverty and desperation of their constituents; many have already taken steps to quash dissent. Trust me when I say things won't end well if they aren't regularly replaced with new, democratically elected representatives. This can even happen in really great countries that have leaders who genuinely want the best for their nation and their people.

One example of a country that is *not* heading in the right direction despite the quality of both its leadership and its people is China. With China set to become the world's largest economy and with many first-world democracies in crisis, a number of other countries may be lured into following China's lead, politically. Since China will be looking to secure its sphere of influence over the next few decades, many global leaders are concerned that we may be heading toward another Cold War, this time with China pitted against Europe and the United States.

That said, let's address why the Chinese political and economic models are not set up to succeed in the long term.

CHINA'S SHALLOW SUCCESS AND PERILOUS FUTURE

China has experienced record economic growth over the past two decades. But, as its trade surplus begins to shrink and the real estate bubble that has been building for years eventually bursts, the country's economic outlook is becoming questionable. Add to that civil unrest from pro-democracy groups and oppressed ethnic minorities and it becomes apparent that the next decades are going to test the resilience of Chinese governance.

Considering the many shortcomings of non-democratic governance that's not benefitting from peaceful revolutions at the top, things are currently looking pretty bleak for the country as a whole, unless...

There is no doubt that the past twenty years have been years of Chinese ascendancy. As industrialized nations developed a taste for inexpensive consumer goods, China began its rise to industrial supremacy by leveraging its roughly one billion-strong labor force. The Chinese work ethic is famous around the world, and Chinese factory workers only strengthened this reputation, working back-breakingly long shifts in the numerous manufacturing centers the Chinese government set up over the past two decades. In 2014, China even overtook the United States as the world's largest economy (at least in terms of purchasing power).

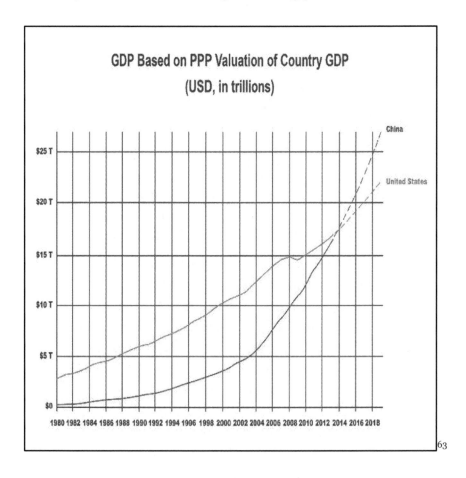

63

Human rights organizations have often decried working conditions in many of the factories that fueled China's rise; recently, even companies like Apple were caught in scandals involving Chinese workers putting in so many hours assembling their products that they regularly fell asleep inside the factories in which they work. Despite working conditions, many of the one billion men and women that comprise China's workforce have benefited greatly from the country's growth. As mentioned earlier, the falling poverty rate in China over the past twenty years has been the primary driver of the reduced global poverty rate.

But there are very serious troubles ahead for China which must be addressed if the country is to have any chance of long term success. One of China's many brilliant philosophers, Confucius, said, "By three methods we may learn wisdom: first, by reflection, which is noblest; second, by imitation, which is easiest; and third by experience, which is bitterest."

Reflecting on Recent History

In the first part of the 20th century, the Chinese people spent many years fighting to change their country. In 1949, after nearly two decades of extremely violent internal conflict, Chairman of the Chinese Communist Party Mao Tse-tung founded the People's Republic of China based on his own interpretation of Marxist communism. Despite noble goals, a history of very enlightened intellectuals, and access to some of the world's premier intellectuals, for the subsequent half century China saw relatively little growth.

A number of factors contributed to China's sluggish expansion. In 1956, a few years after the end of the Korean War, one of Mao's devious schemes saw the Chinese government encourage intellectuals throughout the country to publish their thoughts on how the country could be improved. Under the pretense of enhancing governance and making the country run more efficiently, the Hundred Flowers Campaign inspired many of China's most influential thinkers to contribute their ideas to a vibrant national discussion. However, once their opinions were made public, many of these intellectuals were arrested and never heard from again.

A few years later, after purging dissent from much of China and consolidating his power, Mao dragged the country along on another misguided attempt to bring it more in line with his communist ideal: the Great Leap Forward. This plan saw massive plots of Chinese farmland taken from their owners and formed into huge, communal farms. This redistribution resulted in two near totally failed harvests that led to the entire country's food supply dwindling to nearly nothing. While the full scope of the damage done to China by the Great Leap Forward is not completely understood because of how secretive the nation was at the time, it's roughly estimated that between twenty-five and fifty million Chinese died of starvation and diseases brought on by malnutrition.

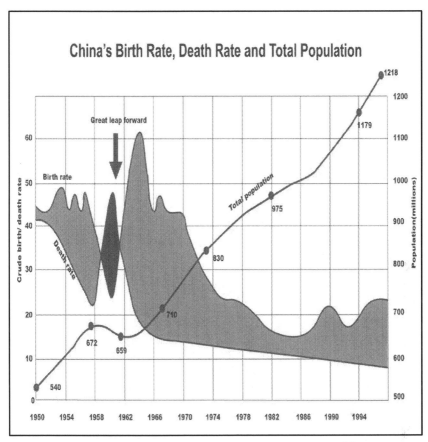

Source: Barcelona Field Studies Centre[64]

Despite being discredited by his ill-conceived policies and divisive political strategies, Mao made a number of efforts to cement his power over the next two decades. Nevertheless, when he died in 1976, he left behind what many consider to be a legacy of failure. In 1980, new Chinese leadership began to open the country up to the West and initiated some incremental reforms to the country's political system.

These reforms led to small improvements in the country, but, when pro-democracy protests were staged in Tiananmen Square in 1989, they were described as "counter-revolutionary riots" by the government and were brutally suppressed by troops and armored vehicles. The clampdown resulted in the deaths of many protestors. This pushed China back into old habits, with many pro-democracy activists arrested and a number of security and government officials "removed" from their positions. The resulting global outrage damaged China's international relations and hurt its economy. Reforms did not begin again for three years.

Imitating Success

In the mid-1990s, the march of globalization began to open China to the world, as first-world workers transitioned to post-industrial jobs, and the supply of cheap labor in industrialized nations dried up. In 2001, China was welcomed into the World Trade Organization (WTO), complete with all the benefits of membership: reduced trade tariffs; fewer travel restrictions; and easier international business transactions, to name just a few. The Chinese government then decided to imitate the industrial economies of the First World by guiding its economy toward an enormous expansion of the industrial sector. To a large degree, this mimicked the strategies of Western countries and followed in their successful footsteps.

This strategy actually turned out to be one of the best economic decisions China's leadership could have made, as it was the best way to leverage its gargantuan but relatively unskilled workforce. In the years since, the strategy has paid large dividends for the country, creating many millionaires and increasing China's gross domestic product by *hundreds* of percentage points.

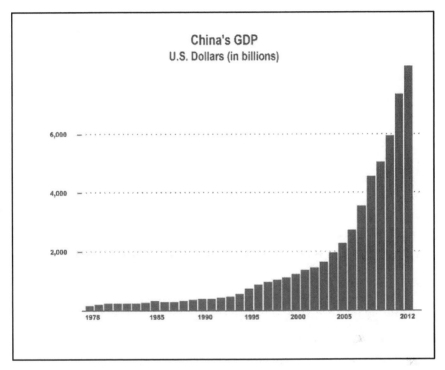

Source: Harvard Business Review via World Bank[65]

Additionally, huge international mega-corporations from industrialized nations lined up to build and operate factories in China in which they could produce goods very inexpensively. While Chinese factories were only able to produce and assemble low tech goods at first, the Chinese economy evolved quickly to the point where many of the world's most cutting-edge technology companies are now assembling their highly complex goods in Chinese factories.

As years passed, China's trade surplus with western nations climbed to tens of billions of dollars each year.

But now, the time for imitation has ended. As China's population becomes more educated, manufacturing jobs are losing their appeal, and citizens are demanding reforms that create more higher-paying white-collar opportunities for a larger percentage of people. The exhausting, endless hours of manual labor are no longer something that many Chinese want to be part of. As a result, civil unrest has increased and calls for a more democratic government that is better able to adjust to the demands of the global economy and the needs of the Chinese people are becoming louder every year.

Bitter Experience

China's economy is currently absolutely dependent on the success of its industrial sector and exports to first-world nations. Nearly half of China's GDP is generated by industrial fields such as construction, manufacturing, and power generation, as a consequence.

One of the reasons this situation hasn't already created more problems for China is that, despite relatively low pay, its labor force is able to afford basic goods and services, in large part as a result of the byproducts and cast offs from the country's export-oriented domestic manufacturing. Additionally, piracy of name brand products and services in China is rampant, with copyright and trademark laws seeming not to apply in many areas of the country.

As we already discussed earlier in this book, the unstoppable march of technology makes a greater number of

Chinese manufacturing jobs obsolete every year. The eventual result of this trend is that China will require fewer and fewer workers to meet export demand, as time passes. This problem is exacerbated by the fact that China's middle class has not yet been firmly established by the country's industrial economy. Currently, millions of Chinese still live on meager incomes and have accumulated very little in savings.

If technological unemployment eliminates the need for huge numbers of Chinese workers, there is a real danger that the resulting unemployment will cause severe social and political instability. We've already seen evidence from the recent events in Hong Kong that, despite its not having as violent a reaction as it did at Tiananmen Square, the Chinese government is still not exactly welcoming to new ideas about modernizing the ways that the country is run.

One other well documented issue that soon will come to a head is the construction boom. It has created huge, empty ghost towns throughout China. Each one contains thousands of behemoth apartment buildings and commercial structures with few or no inhabitants and customers.

A running joke going around the construction industry in China these days is that you just have to build the outside of new structures, because the investors who buy them never bother to look inside the homes and commercial buildings they purchase. The joke would be more humorous if it weren't for the fact that thousands of buildings that are nowhere near habitable have already been sold to investors as finished products.

As investors start to wise up to what's going on and confirm the fact that there is nobody in China who can afford to buy the shoddily built apartments on which they've spent hundreds of millions of dollars, China will be in the midst of a real estate bubble that is long overdue to burst. There is growing international concern about this. While few experts agree one hundred percent on what will happen if it does burst, the worst case scenarios predict that millions of Chinese construction workers will lose their jobs, as nearly the entire construction industry grinds to a halt.

Further aggravating tensions within China is serious and continuing unrest in the giant Xinjiang province, the sprawling northwest region of the country. The ethnic Uyghur population has chafed under Chinese rule, violence has increased, and subsequent government crackdowns have resulted in many deaths. While an uneasy peace has been established, analysts worry that Xinjiang is just one more Chinese powder keg waiting for the right spark to ignite it.

Mourners hold a candlelight vigil for victims of an attack by alleged Xinxiang separatists[66]

With all these challenges, the Chinese government is going to have to adapt quickly to changing circumstances and be open to new ideas and ways of doing things if it is going to survive in its current form. *And this is something that it is completely unequipped to do.*

The people who have risen to power in China have done so largely to their own benefit. Corruption is rife within the Party. Needless to say, this inspires little confidence in the Chinese people or in foreign observers that, when faced with huge, national issues, the government will react in a way that focuses on the best interests of the entire country.

There is a real and growing pessimism among many economists, analysts, and other experts that, if unrest in China rises to the point where the people in power feel that their lifestyles or powerbase are being threatened, then, despite international pressure, the government will fall back into its authoritarian ways. This is because, as we discussed in a previous chapter, once leaders are allowed to stay in power too long they become addicted to the perks and lifestyle that that power allows them to acquire.

There is still some hope that China can avoid disaster, but I believe it's a faint hope. Over the last two decades, a colossal web of power, revenue relationships, and dependencies have quickly and permanently formed, extracting significant opportunities out of the economy and away from China's citizens. As we discussed, once it gets going, it's hard to untangle the giant web of corruption.

And, as we also discussed, even if *intentional corruption* could somehow be near-eradicated (as current President Xi Jinping is attempting to do), without a regular and systematic change in the power structure and people at the top—facilitated only by fair and transparent elections—*unintentional corruption* will persist to equally destructive effect.

My heart goes out to the Chinese people. They are a great people with a strong sense of their rich history and rightful place in the 21st-century world. So it's only a matter of time until they achieve freedom; it's not a question of if but a question of when. To paraphrase John F. Kennedy again, those that would block peaceful revolutions only make violent revolution inevitable. So the only questions are whether the current government can take the very difficult measures that are required and, if not, how disruptive the coming revolution will be. When the time comes, the Chinese people will step up, they will be courageous and they will get freedom. I just hope the price they'll have to pay—in terms of blood, heartache, and loss of momentum to their economy and society—won't be devastatingly high.

The surest way for China to avoid regressing into deeper authoritarianism and the revolution that will inevitably follow would be for the government to massively increase transparency and the pace of democratic reforms—allowing for *peaceful revolutions* at the top—and to take giant steps to address the nation's growing inequality. Without taking these steps, China's future is in real peril. This is because poverty and inequality don't just create terrible governments; they also often have even more destructive consequences.

POVERTY AND INEQUALITY BREED EXTREMISM AND TERRORISM

When people have nothing to lose in their current lives, extreme ideologies and promises of a perfect afterlife have a much greater appeal. This often makes them easy targets for groups with radical ideologies and seemingly simple answers to complicated questions.

As radical groups consolidate their power in much the same way dictators would, the key factors of poverty and inequality once again create monsters that can do almost immeasurable damage to their own countries and to the rest of the world.

Though the trucks, filled to the brim with heavily armed men who formed the new authority, rolled into town only a year ago, it seemed as if decades had passed since their arrival. The ferocious battles that raged outside the city before spilling over into its streets had left scars on the landscape that had yet to heal. Buildings turned to rubble by the fierce, bloody war still lay in ruins, despite promises from the new authority that they would be rebuilt.

Bullet and grenade holes in those structures still standing bore testament to the viciousness of battles that thundered from one street to the next. The people of the city had also suffered during the war, with many families struggling to recover from losing loved ones who had either fought in the conflict or been caught in the middle of it. Once the new authority took over, it had spared few of the prisoners it held, often choosing to make very public displays of their bloody executions.

At first, the people had been cautiously optimistic about the new authority; many people had even joined them to fight against the old leaders. In the years prior to the authority's arrival, chaos, crime, and poverty had run rampant throughout the entire region.

The collapse of the old regime many years before had created a power vacuum; warlords and crime bosses had been only too eager to fill it. These power hungry men had possessed no interest in leading the people or governing, only in power and control. As a result, violence, malnutrition, and outright starvation had eventually become part of daily city life for those not connected to the right people.

In the years that preceded the takeover by the new authority, people had believed it would be impossible for their lives to get any harder. So, when the new authority promised them law, order, and the chance to serve a higher purpose, many residents of the city had flocked to their cause.

When the new authority took over, they quickly made it known that things would be done in new, very precise ways. There were no alternatives to their fanatical belief system, and, for those brave, stupid, or careless enough to disobey the new authority's rules, punishment was swift and... decisive.

As the people slowly realized that they had welcomed a monster into their city with open arms, it was already too late. While the criminality and chaos that plagued the region was reduced, the corruption and cruelty of the new authority was, in many ways, much worse. Nobody left alive had the power or the will to fight anymore, and the population began to resign themselves once again to all-too-familiar lives of poverty and hopelessness.

It seemed as if men with guns had always run the country. Whether they wore uniforms or traditional garb, they were always easy to spot, because nearly every one of them walked around the place like he owned it. Perhaps they did own it. Surely nobody would be foolish enough to argue with them now, if they made such a claim.

As months passed and the new authority consolidated its power, it was the women of the city who began to suffer the most. As they went about their daily routines, they were subjected to the abuse of the new authority's "law" enforcers. Essentially thugs with chips on their shoulders, these enforcers made clear their disdain for those who didn't belong to their organization (if you could even call it that). Beatings were a daily occurrence and resistance only made things terribly, sometimes even fatally, worse.

Even the activities that had, in the past, allowed the people temporarily to escape their lives of misery were now banned under the new authority. Drinking was no longer allowed, and breweries and taverns had been burnt to ash. Even music and dance were now proscribed, with many former entertainers either moving away or being forced to become beggars and transients, as their only real skill became outlawed.

Hope was a thing of the distant past, and nobody expected anything to ever improve. Things only got worse in the city, never better.

The Rise and Fall of the Taliban

The cheerful story above has a lot in common with the story about how dictators rise, but it's important to examine the ways that some countries devolve to a point where even brutal dictators can't (or won't) effectively govern them. After many years of poverty and conflict, some parts of the world have grown so chaotic that they have become fundamentally ungovernable without extreme foreign intervention. The population has lost all trust in any government authority, and, as a result, the "best" that the people who live in these regions can hope for is that whatever organization grabs power is less brutal and oppressive than the last.

One example of such a story is that of the Taliban in Afghanistan.

The Soviet occupation of Afghanistan ended in 1989, and, when the Soviets retreated from the country, a power vacuum was created. This vacuum was filled largely by the local warlords who had sprung up to repulse the Soviet occupation.

The warlords (unsurprisingly) were not very peaceful or law-abiding fellows, and they managed to foster an environment in which violence, criminal activity, and corruption were accepted as everyday occurrences. Under the warlords, the vast majority of Afghan people became desperately poor. And, except for those who were lucky enough to belong to the Warlords' inner circles, many Afghans suffered from malnutrition and extreme poverty. This situation continued for a couple of years until the Taliban moved up from the south of the country to assert control over the entire nation.

The Taliban, a movement comprised of primarily ethnic Pashtun fighters, committed to taking control of Afghanistan in the early 1990s. In 1994, they moved from their southern bases to assault and, ultimately, control the major Afghan city of Kandahar. Over the next three years, the Taliban achieved victory over the only remaining band of Afghan warlords, known as the Northern Alliance. After the Alliance's defeat, in very short order, the Taliban ended up controlling the capital of Afghanistan, Kabul, along with the vast majority of the countryside.

Once in power, they implemented a strict interpretation of Sharia law that banned music, alcohol, dancing, and a variety of other activities they deemed in violation of their religious strictures. Women were denied education, employment, and many other basic elements of civilization, while also being forced to wear body-covering vestments known as *burqas*.

They committed a number of cultural and humanitarian outrages which garnered international condemnation but very little recrimination. Eventually, the Taliban provided safe harbor for Osama Bin Laden's terrorist network, Al Qaeda, which went on to perpetrate a number of international terror attacks, including, most infamously, the September 11 terror attacks against the United States.

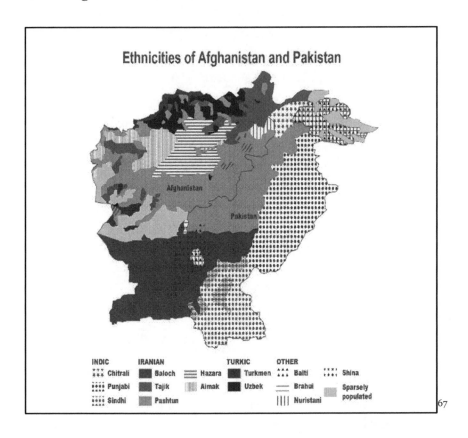

Following the September 11 attacks, the Taliban were driven from power by the U.S. and an international military coalition. Although heavily outgunned by international forces, many senior Taliban and Al Qaeda leaders were able to flee to the Tora Bora cave fortress in southern Afghanistan. Due to mismanagement of forces by the coalition high commanders, many Taliban and Al Qaeda leaders, including the infamous Osama Bin Laden, managed to escape south into Pakistan. The Taliban went on to reestablish themselves in the areas straddling the Afghanistan/Pakistan border. In spite of international efforts to root them out or negotiate a peace, the Taliban continue campaigns of suicide bombings and attacks on civilians to this day.

While the Taliban may be the most recognizable group that owes a large part of its success to poverty, there are others to choose from. Boko Haram in Africa and Daesh (also known as ISIS and ISIL) in the Middle East are just a couple of existing groups that share similar tales. The number of extremist organizations throughout history that have taken advantage of poverty to swell their ranks is nearly countless.

This is because people who become hopeless due to poverty are much easier to lure into joining extremist organizations if they stand even a small chance of improving their lives. Folks who have nothing to lose *risk* nothing, except lives they hate, when they join these groups. Fundamentalist ideology that offers simple answers to why people's lives are so hard and what they need to do to improve them is a lot more appealing to the poor and disenfranchised. This opinion is shared by a number of world leaders, including U.S. Secretary of State John Kerry, who recently said, "...poverty [is] in many cases...the root cause of terrorism or even the root cause of the disenfranchisement of millions of people on this planet."[68]

This is probably why, despite thousands of first-world Islamic extremists traveling overseas to wage jihad, a very small percentage of them become suicide bombers. Violence, extremism, and the willingness to sacrifice one's life for the promise of paradise aren't rooted in Islamic teachings; they are rooted in poverty and disenfranchisement.

The Extremist/Terrorist Playbook

I've already covered the dictator playbook. The extremist playbook isn't much different. I'll quickly summarize:

Step One: *Poverty and the lack of opportunity and purpose screws up a country royally,* destroying any chance of democratic governance.

Step Two: *A new, fanatically dedicated group moves in* and tells the poor and disenfranchised masses that it feels their pain and can help them solve their problems.

Step Three: Because of their popular appeal, their promises of many different forms of salvation, and their ability to create fear in those that oppose them, *the group rises to power.*

Step Four: *The group gains enough support that it's able to wipe out all dissenters* and censor all those who don't agree with its beliefs.

Step Five: As the group consolidates its position, it *concentrates as much wealth and as many resources as it can* within its own ranks, creating even greater poverty than before it rose to power.

This process eventually leads to another extremist group with a slightly different ideology rousing the masses once again, and the whole process repeats itself.

◆◆◆

At empowr, we operate under the belief that poverty is a major root cause of not only totalitarian governments, but also of the proliferation of terrorist groups and extremist ideology. This means that **eradicating poverty is critically important to the future success of our world**, especially in poorer regions. If you remove poverty, the Poverty Loop is short-circuited, and countries are allowed to grow peacefully and reach their full, democratic potential.

The remainder of this book is dedicated to explaining exactly how we plan to make a contribution toward attacking poverty on a global basis and spreading democracy internationally.

INTRODUCING empowr: THE DEMOCRATIC SOCIAL ECONOMY

empowr is the culmination of years of hard work and seemingly endless cycles of trial, error, and improvement. It's an online platform that leverages the most valuable aspects of social media, online education, entrepreneurialism, and network technology to create an economy that focuses on creating income for the people who actually generate the revenue, rather than on further enriching a small minority of corporate shareholders.

By leveraging powerful, proprietary network technologies, empowr will incorporate billions of people into a social media platform that teaches them new, valuable online skills while helping them to monetize the online activities they already participate in, starting on the very first day they join.

By doing so, we plan on empowering people around the world to make enough money from the platform that they can drastically improve their lives.

empowr is a huge technology, sociology, and economic experiment that has been in development for the past fifteen years, building on top of my own prior thirteen years of knowledge, gained from the school of hard knocks by building various community, educational, and monetization technologies and companies. The software programs behind the platform are highly complex creations that contain countless lines of programming code, meticulously implemented by nearly 1,000 computer scientists and engineers and some of the most innovative online technology ever invented, as evidenced by numerous broad patents issued by the United States Patent and Trademark Office (USPTO).

At the time of this writing in August 2015, only days before the launch of the "open alpha" phase of the empowr platform, many components of the platform have been carefully tested and vetted over multiple years by over 100,000 incredibly selfless "closed alpha" test users located in every single country in the world.

That said the platform's major building blocks are things with which nearly everyone is likely familiar.

So what is a Democratic Social Economy?

I'll go into more detail later on, but for now you should know that there are three overarching ideas that comprise empowr:

- ➢ **Democratic** in the way that the business is administered and run. Rather than be accountable exclusively to shareholders, empowr instead gives *customers* the strongest voice in company decisions, by allowing them to elect empowr's highest level executive (its president) and guide other company officials and thereby influence the business's direction in a manner similar to democratic countries long ago. The result is a much more agile company, one that is able to move in unison with its customer's desires and react to their ideas, hopes, complaints, and dissatisfactions. We believe that, when the person at the helm of a company is elected by its customers (as opposed to the shareholders), she will be much better equipped to prioritize employees' work around those things that matter most to her customers. The result will be customer centricity elevated to levels never seen before, and will translate into more satisfied customers and a series of strategic advantages over competitors.

  Even the most "profit driven" shareholders will benefit from this approach, just like the richest landowners ending up benefitting grandly from the formation of inclusive democracies around the world. When customer centricity and engagement explode, so do corporate profits; empowr invests these profits right back into the platform and its citizens, which will create a virtuous circle that further builds the company's revenues, profits and value to its customers.

Democratic also describes an overarching concept around how empowr's products and services were designed from the ground up. For example, our flagship advertising platform (*called Democratized Ads)* has been designed to allow someone with no funds or credit whatsoever, to use thousands of dollars in high quality advertising, only paying the company for those ads in the future out of their profits when (and only if) they are able to.

In a similar fashion, our *Democratized Marketplace* allows those with no capital to improve their lives by effectively taking control of a large amount of product or service inventory to build a strong recurring stream of profits for themselves, starting with absolutely no capital, products or services of their own.

And, of course, empowr's *educational system*, as we will discuss soon, is nothing if not democratic, giving students the freedom to choose their teachers after reviewing powerful but easy-to-understand teacher performance criteria. It gives teachers the limitless freedom to earn as much—and improve their lives as far—as their motivation, creativity, and passion will take them.

> **Social** interaction between empowr's customers is essential because of the rapid pace at which its citizens need to acquire the important skills required for them to become productive members of the empowr economy. Every new empowr member is systematically introduced to more experienced members, starting at the moment they join. These more experienced members (who volunteer to become teachers) become fully accountable to the new member's learning and growth. This process also encourages innovation, critical thinking, elevated productivity, and entrepreneurialism.

> A vibrant **Economy** is what allows members to become productive members of the community—with many specialized roles available for members to participate in and earn from. From the very first moment customers join empowr, they are able to monetize (which means earn from) the very same online social activities that most of them already participate in on other social websites (such as posting and sharing photos, videos, blogs, and other content).

   Gradually, a combination of human and technological elements help to gently handhold and upgrade the members' skills and capabilities—and purchasing power—until such time that each member becomes an important contributor to the production, distribution, and consumption of products and services—which is the very definition of an economy. As members learn new skills, the value of their participation in the online economy grows, as does their income. And, so do the platform's revenues and profits, which empowr injects right back into the platform, helping to further elevate members' incomes, opportunities, and standard of living.

These three key aspects of empowr are why my team and I call the platform we've created *the **Democratic Social Economy** or **DSE***. Each element of empowr works synergistically with the other elements to create an experience that can be incredibly rewarding for the people who participate. By giving members (called "citizens" in empowr) control over how they generate revenue as well as over the policies and institutions that govern every aspect of the platform, the DSE aims to revolutionize the way people around the world work and produce, learn and improve, play and consume.

Perhaps as importantly, for many citizens of the platform, empowr is their first opportunity to participate in a functioning, inclusive democracy where their vote and rights are protected, their social mobility potential is nonfictional, and they feel like they have a real chance to improve their lives and that of their loved ones without fear, intimidation, or the need to sell out to ideologies, causes, or groups they don't believe in.

A Day in the Life of an empowr User

Let me paint a picture for you of how I see things in the future. Let's fast forward a few years and imagine that empowr has attracted a huge user base, with millions or even billions of people participating each day in the Democratic Social Economy.

Let's think of a model user. We'll call her Corina. Corina wakes up and starts her day by logging into her empowr account to check the news and to look in on how her latest online enterprise is going. The first thing she checks is to see, while she was sleeping, how much money she made from the products, services, and digital goods that she offers within the platform.

To her delight, it turns out that one of the ads she created for a product that is offered by another empowr citizen generated thirty-four clicks overnight, and three of those clicks resulted in sales. Since each sale generates nearly $100 for her, she had a productive night's sleep! (On empowr, a citizen can easily create ads for any product or service that's available on the platform and automatically share in the profits the very moment the ads succeed in generating revenues.)

Corina is also a blogger and is excited to learn that people are enjoying the blog post she wrote the day before, based on how many times it has already been shared! She is also pleasantly surprised to see that one of her favorite celebrities has liked and shared one of her blogs. It's quite a good start to the day, but things only get better.

It turns out that one of the auctions she set up the other day closed while she was asleep; a friendly-looking user from France paid a great price for the iPad she'd put on sale only twelve hours before. (Within empowr, auctions typically move very quickly empowr because of how tightly integrated the marketplace is in its social network; but such a quick turnaround for a 25% profit is really encouraging for Corina.) It's helpful that all members can bid directly on items they see in their feeds, without leaving their feed or needing to add funds. (They are almost all earning from various sources.) In addition, if they don't have any funds whatsoever, the platform will actually allow them to purchase an item and immediately turn around and resell the item to produce a profit. The ability to generate profits in the marketplace, starting with no capital, products or services to offer, is why empowr's marketplace is called "democratized."

After checking to make sure the money from her auction sale was deposited in her empowr balance, Corina checks her inbox to find it filled with congratulations for how her writing has taken off from her success coach, her friends, and her colleagues in the blogosphere. Corina previously worked with many of the wonderful people who have sent her congratulatory messages, but she is still a bit overwhelmed by the outpouring of support.

In a giving mood, Corina decides to visit some of her fans' pages to see if there is anything she can share or purchase. She notices that one fan is currently running a contest to promote a new app they created that gives empowr citizens a way to contribute toward the building of a hospital in rural Cambodia. Touched by the fans' ingenuity and generosity, Corina donates $5 to the cause with a click of her mouse.

There's an election going on within the platform to decide who will be the next president of empowr, so Corina takes some time to check the most recent polls. She has her hopes set on an Indian economist from the University of Mumbai who she thinks has very good ideas about expanding the marketplace features to include even more services than it already offers. As she reads the latest polls, she's happy to see that, even with a long list of qualified candidates running for office, her Indian economist is managing to maintain a respectable lead. Corina can't wait to see the platform's new direction, if he's elected.

Corina realizes that, in all her excitement, she forgot all about breakfast. She quickly turns to the empowr directory of services and orders a lunch delivery from a local Mexican restaurant. Since the restaurant accepts payments from empowr and even provides empowr citizens with instant discounts, she can't help but smile as she realizes that lunch is "free," thanks to the profits she made overnight via her ads, blogs, and the sale of the iPad (which she had purchased—without using her own money—to resell only the day before).

Corina has been working hard on her writing and on expanding her various empowr revenue streams, so she is looking forward to taking a vacation somewhere warm. It is winter in Vancouver, Canada, where Corina lives most of the year, and she's decided that there's only so much freezing weather that even a Canadian can take without a little break. With that in mind, Corina loads up one of the travel services that are integrated into the empowr economy.

Inspired by lunch, Corina decides to look at some flights down to Mexico and does a little research on which towns and resorts have the best reviews. As it turns out, a few of the people with whom she's connected on empowr have reviewed a particular resort that is twenty miles from Cancun, Mexico, at the tip of the Yucatan peninsula. Apparently the beaches there are beyond gorgeous, and the people there are super-friendly to tourists. It would be nice to actually meet some of her fans in Mexico who have helped her earn, as well as those she has assisted. Corina always makes a point of breaking bread with some of her fans when she travels, as she sees that as a great way to make her trips more fun and stimulating. One side benefit of these meetings is that they also tend to boost her business.

The resort offers discounts to empowr users who agree to review the resort online after their stay. Since Corina loves a good deal, she buys one of the packages that include daily activities and a fully inclusive five-night stay. She splurges and gets a beach-front room—the photos she will take of the sunrises and sunsets will surely pay for themselves, as they spread through empowr and her networks of fans. She books her flight and room for four weeks away, knowing that the next month is going to go by *very* slowly.

As Corina decides to work on her next blog post, she puts on the custom music mix she purchased from a fan, smiles, and realizes that she's already counting the days until she gets to go play on the beach.

What Else Will empowr Do?

One of the really great things about the empowr platform is that it's designed to grow with the citizen base and with the businesses that choose to use it. Even as I write this, my team and I are working on new and more efficient ways to integrate new services from third party companies into the platform.

In the future, perhaps nearly every aspect of people's lives will be managed from within the empowr platform. As we make it easier every day for people to join and participate in the platform, the possibilities of where we can go are nearly endless.

The integration of the empowr platform with third-party developers, brick-and-mortar businesses, and local services will enable citizens to use their empowr earnings anywhere and anyhow: from paying for their apartment rent to taking a cooking class or purchasing something as simple as toilet paper. Having access to your daily earnings in the palm of your hand not only makes life much more convenient, but it also allows people greater purchasing power because the cost of transactions is almost completely eliminated.

One of the most interesting recent developments here in the U.S. is the expansion of our healthcare system. Perhaps someday people will be able to look for doctors on a fully integrated healthcare platform that tracks not only patients' reviews of their doctors, but also how healthy each patient is after seeing a particular doctor. The best surgeons will be able to highlight how successful the vast majority of their procedures have been, and users will be able pick medical providers based on their particular needs. It is one of our ambitions to offer free healthcare to all empowr citizens eventually, as we believe that healthier citizens will ultimately add more to the platform economically than the amount it will cost.

As we grow, we expect many traditional businesses to participate fully in the platform, integrating their products and services into empowr's structure.

Further, as we expand the educational aspects of our platform, we hope to offer all our citizens cutting-edge classes on some of the most valuable topics in the world. Because we are so passionate about the accountability of everyone who offers services within our platform, all classes will be taught by professors whose students can review every aspect of what they were taught and provide feedback on how to make each class even better. Potential students will even be able to track the performance of an integrated online educational institution's graduates, and chart their course in the economy following graduation.

empowr's fully integrated political system will evolve every year, along with the platform. New candidates will become interested in running for office in the next election cycle, and the new ideas and energy they bring to the business will increase the company's efficiency *and* improve citizen engagement.

◆◆◆

Of course, I dream about *all* of this stuff, but I don't want you to think I'm getting too terribly full of myself. I realize that we have a *long* way to go before a few of the things I've described have a chance to become reality. I also realize that we are most definitely going to have a ton of competitors popping up, once more entrepreneurs realize the potential for what we're doing. In fact, I'm counting on it.

One of the ongoing themes throughout this book has been that competition is one of the biggest drivers behind successful businesses and organizations. When companies grow so large that they snuff out all competitors, they inevitably get fat, dumb, and lazy.

That's something I don't want for empowr.

That's why we openly share so many of our proprietary technologies and, in part, is why I've written this book. I welcome competition, because I know it drives our team to be the absolute best they can be. I think that, by pushing us to innovate and think of new and better ideas to add to the platform, healthy competition will be really good for us in the long term.

The bottom line, however, is that I do *want us to win by taking advantage of the Network Effect,* because I believe that our winning is important to the success of our overall mission of fighting poverty and, more generally, of using technology to make the world a better place.

I worry that the other companies that pop up to challenge empowr won't be half as dedicated to (or capable of, due to their shareholder requirements and corporate governance structure) addressing the world problems that I describe in this book. Like the vast majority of other businesses that have been created over the course of history, I expect that most or all companies that compete with empowr will be concerned primarily with squeezing and extracting as much profit from their users as they can, so that they keep their shareholders happy.

As a result, if empowr does fail, the company that steps in to fill the inevitable online "power vacuum" likely won't share our ideals or commitment to democracy, transparency, and accountability. And that will likely be very bad for the entire online community. Probably bad for the world, as well.

That's why my team and I have worked under some difficult conditions and committed so many years of our lives to enabling a business strategy that, we believe, has set empowr up for the successful fulfillment of its mission and goals.

STRATEGICALLY LEVERAGING THE NETWORK EFFECT

Our Strategy: Leverage the Network Effect for everyday people by building an inclusive economy in empowr (as opposed to extractive); carefully democratizing the two main revenue and value drivers of most successful websites (the company's Advertising platform and its Marketplace); further growing social mobility through a revolutionary Educational system; and democratizing the company itself so profits are not removed but returned to the people to further grow the empowr economy and empowr's management is most accountable to its citizens as opposed to its shareholders.

Along with making a dent in global poverty, as a result of our trial and errors we also hope to spread new ideas about how to use technology to reform

educational systems and governments around the world.

While in the upcoming chapters I describe in more detail empowr's approach to poverty, education, and governance problems, this chapter is dedicated to explaining succinctly how empowr will use the Network Effect to help address each individual problem. The primary reason for addressing the Network Effect independently is because it's an incredibly powerful technological force that has a big impact on every one of empowr's main goals.

As I described earlier, the Network Effect is one of the most potent forces modern technology has brought to the world. Already, we've seen many giant corporations successfully leverage it to dominate their fields of business. Bearing this in mind, my team and I have formulated a strategy that is specifically designed to take full advantage of the Network Effect in order to expand our customer base, grow the business, and increase revenues.

This, in turn, will allow empowr to play a role in addressing major global problems such as poverty and inequality, dysfunctional educational systems, highly inefficient governments, the erosion of democracy, extremism and terrorism. This may seem like an unbelievably lofty goal and, truth be told, without the Network Effect it might not be possible. However, *with* the Network Effect, that lofty goal becomes achievable.

empowr might be the first business built from the ground up to use the advantage of the Network Effect to address poverty on a global scale. Because of this fact, we'll approach tackling poverty in a way that has never been tried before. One reason we are going to be the first business to successfully use network technology to tackle global poverty is that, in the past, access to the Internet has simply not been widespread enough.

But with the expansion of wireless network technology, the Internet is adding well over a hundred million first-time users each year. By giving these first-time users the opportunity to participate immediately in our Democratic Social Economy and start earning right off the bat, we will see exponential growth in our customer base and revenue streams.

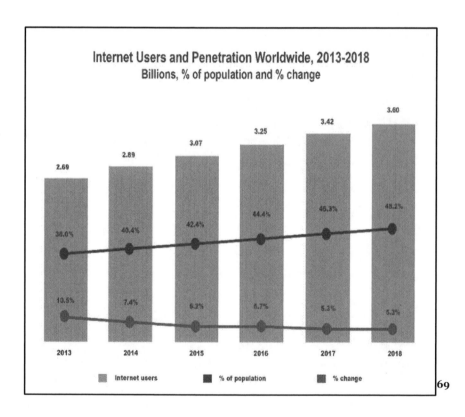

69

While we return almost all of this revenue to citizens, we will also continue to channel revenue into improving the platform and expanding the services we offer our customers, all with an eye toward increasing the average empowr citizen's earnings. That's our goal.

Education is another of the fields to which empowr will contribute by using the Network Effect. Our educational platform is very focused on educating users on how to increase the value of their skills within the platform itself, and provides them with top notch instructors. We want to trigger a cycle with our educational system that is the exact opposite of the dumbification cycle I described earlier.

The system is set up to have the best teachers offering to our users some of the highest quality education available. As we have the smartest teachers educate the next generation of students, we create a positive feedback loop that creates better teachers *and* more successful students each time it repeats. *Think of the Network Effect's impact on our education platform as a "smartification cycle."*

Don't roll your eyes!

Trust me when I say that it's actually pretty fantastic:

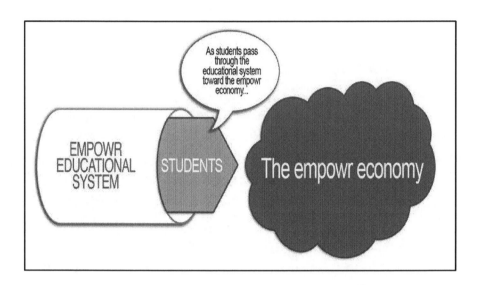

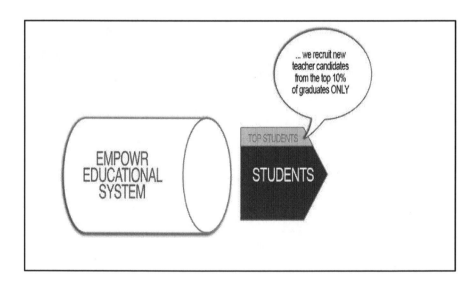

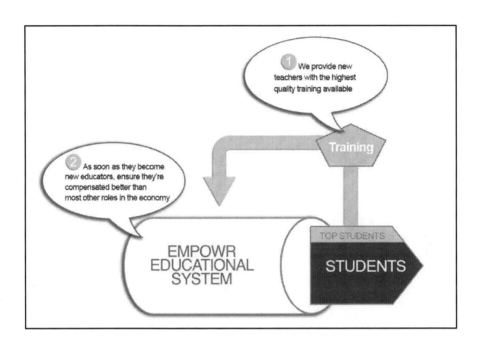

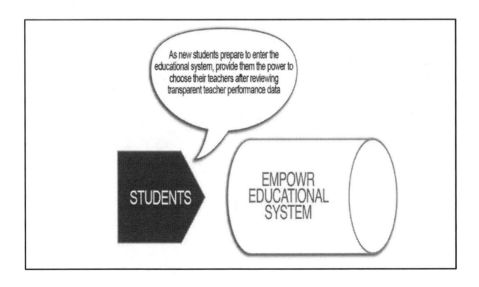

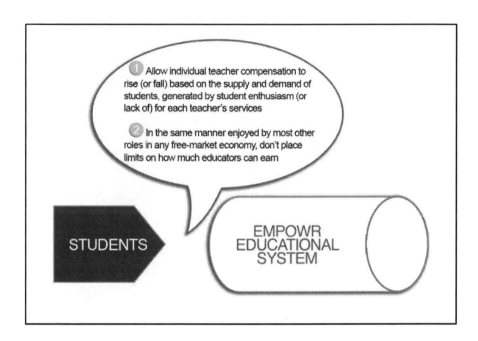

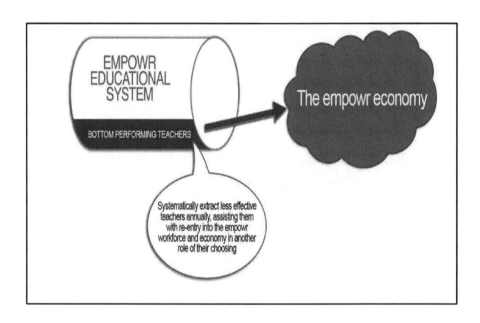

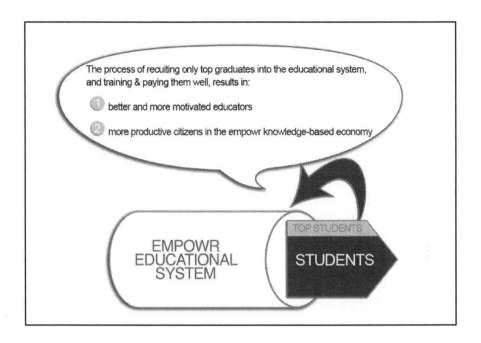

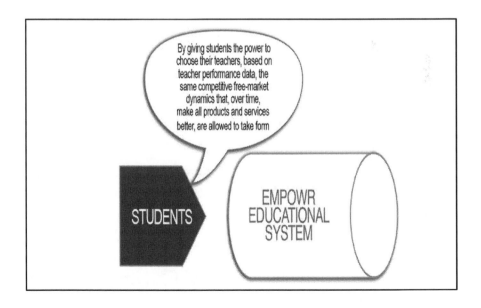

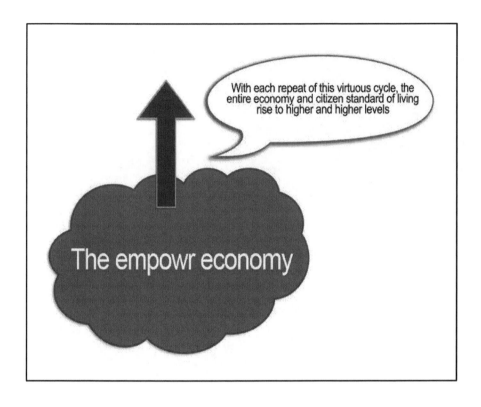

◆ ◆ ◆

empowr will also take advantage of the power of the Network Effect to influence government. The Democratic Social Economy that empowr has created is the first platform of its kind to allow users a chance to vote on the president of the company that controls it, as well as assume the role of president or other political roles. As more people join empowr every year and realize how rewarding it is to *really* have a say in the governance of an organization, enthusiasm for democracy will spread beyond the virtual world. The greater the number of people who find success within empowr, the higher the chances of people becoming believers in the power of democracy and insisting on it for their own countries.

Each major aspect of empowr's strategy is designed to benefit from bringing in more people. When a person joins our community, they not only add independent value to it, but they also make the other citizens who are already a part of the community more valuable to the platform, as well.

The underlying point of all this is that, while the Network Effect is an unbeatable force, it **doesn't have to hurt humanity**. Instead, if we can harness it so that it **helps** the majority of people it touches, our efforts could have an unprecedented positive effect on the world. And, as you have probably guessed already, empowr's plan is to do exactly that. The first problem we'll take on using this strategy is one of this book's major focuses: *poverty*.

empowr's APPROACH TO TACKLING POVERTY

empowr attracts new citizens (users) because it does not require people to learn new skills or have any money to start, while it allows them to monetize their existing skill set. These three factors ensure that there is no barrier to entry.

We do this while maintaining a highly agile platform that's laser-focused on offering merit-based upward mobility.

Our dedication to maintaining zero barriers to entry, running an agile platform, and facilitating upward mobility means empowr will help users make money from the day they join and continue to grow their income as their skills improve. As users increase their income consistently, they will be able to meet more of their basic needs each month until, through their own work, they are able to lift themselves out of poverty.

A million different things cross people's minds when they think about poverty, from tragic images of starving children on the television to the large homeless populations present in some developed nations. This is because, although poverty affects *every* country, it does so in very different ways.

While third-world and developing countries are certainly more likely to have large segments of their population living in severe poverty, even many citizens of first-world countries have trouble providing themselves with sufficient food, clean water, housing and essential medical services. The truth is that poverty is an incredibly complex international issue with enough angles to confuse even the most intelligent person. (Feel free to Google the question if you don't believe me.) That's why I think it will help readers understand empowr's approach to poverty if I quickly explain the aspects of poverty we are most focused on attacking.

Merriam-Webster's dictionary defines poverty as "the state of one who lacks a usual or socially acceptable amount of money or material possessions." While there are certainly other ways to look at the problem, I believe this very basic definition cuts to the core of what poverty really is: *not having enough money to pay for life.*

Regardless of its designation (e.g., dollar, euro, pound, rupee, yen, etc.), the globalized economy has made money an almost universal tool for purchasing the goods necessary to meet one's basic needs. When poverty is thought of as a lack of money, the question of how to *fix poverty* then becomes how to enable people to make *enough money* to maintain an acceptable standard of living. This relatively simple idea is at the core of the empowr's anti-poverty strategy.

What's in a Dollar?

Once we decided to approach poverty from a monetary perspective, we were (unsurprisingly) presented with a long list of ways in which increasing people's income can improve their lives over the short and long term. While poverty is difficult to quantify, by looking at the daily monetary income of people across the globe, one can begin to get a handle on the issue.

For instance, according to the United Nations, 1.2 billion people across the globe live on less than $1.25 (US dollars) a day; half of humanity lives on less than $2.50 a day; and the World Bank estimates that a whopping 80% of humanity lives on less than $10 dollars a day.[70][71] The idea of living on such a meager income is inconceivable to many citizens of industrialized nations. But, as the cost of living is much lower in developing and third-world countries, most people in these countries manage to survive.

The cost of goods and services is a huge part of the cost of living, but prices vary *greatly* from country to country. This makes it difficult to nail down exactly how much more money people need to earn each day in order to purchase the goods and services necessary to provide for their basic physiological needs. Despite this stumbling block, it's clear that, based on the meager amounts of money that billions of people subsist on, enabling them to earn a relatively small amount more per day could *dramatically* improve their lives.

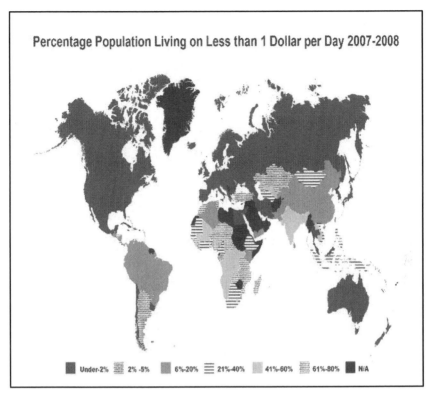

Percentage population living on less than 1 dollar day 2007-2008[72]

By enabling people who live in poverty to earn even just ten or twenty dollars more per day, we can:

- Improve their access to healthcare
- Decrease the percentage of their income they must spend on food
- Help people purchase basic products that improve their productivity
- Increase their access to sanitation, electricity, and clean water
- Help them acquire safer and more secure housing[73]

These improvements are just a few examples of why it is so vitally important to enable people living in poverty to earn more money. That's why my team and I have focused diligently on building a platform and formulating strategies that fight poverty.

But, before we get any deeper into how empowr is addressing poverty, I'd like to clarify where my team and I are coming from. We are *not* delusional, so we are well aware that the platform we've built isn't some magic wand that can be waved to eliminate poverty across the planet. We know that eradicating poverty is a goal that is well beyond the capacity of a single company.

That said, we do believe that, when fully implemented and adopted, our platform will play an important part in helping millions of people worldwide generate the income they need to address many of their basic needs and significantly improve their lives as a result.

When my co-founder Brandie Smith and I were conducting research before officially starting up the empowr project, we found a very interesting and telling relationship between poverty and democracy, which we have since called "the poverty loop": In countries where the median citizen's income was less than $4 per day, democracies only lasted for an average of ten years before failing back into a non-democratic state.

However, when median incomes reach $25 per day, democracies become resilient. Specifically, 34 democracies have existed where median incomes were above $25 per day, and not a single one has failed.

empowr was started with the idea that if, using web and mobile technology, we could deliver to people everywhere both a functional democracy and an economy capable of delivering $25 per day of median citizen income, then perhaps we could help break the global poverty loop in a single generation.

Ultimately, empowr's goal became to help half the world's population, or 4 billion people, earn an average of $25 per day by the year 2025.Let's get to the nuts and bolts of how empowr tackles poverty.

Maintaining Zero Barriers to Entry and Helping Users Monetize Their Existing Skills

People living in poverty have enough hurdles to overcome already, so making empowr *easy* for new people to join and utilize fully has always been one of our top priorities. One way we do this is by eliminating the learning curve that usually comes with joining a new platform. We accomplished this feat by first researching which platforms had already equipped users with online habits or skills.

Over one billion people have been trained very successfully by Facebook, Twitter, and other social media platforms to post and share photos, content, and aspects of their personal lives online. Armed with that knowledge, we designed our user interface to be recognizable immediately to nearly any user who has worked with a social media platform in the past.

Since the vast majority of new empowr citizens already know how to participate in social media, all but the most inexperienced of them swiftly become comfortable with the platform. For the citizens who don't already know how to participate, we created quality video tutorials with an intuitive user interface that make learning these basic online tasks very easy.

Next, we knew that in order to succeed we had to make it so that *no money* was required for new users to join empowr. After all, since poverty is basically a lack of money, how could we expect to lift people *out* of poverty by charging them money up front? That's why we designed our platform from the very start to allow every new user to join and start earning income without having to spend *a dime* of her or his own money to do it.

Because of our efforts toward demolishing any barriers to entry, after users join up at no initial cost, they soon realize they are already skilled enough to use the basic parts of the platform effectively. As their confidence builds, they become increasingly motivated to continue investing time and energy into the platform and to improve their skills.

Eventually citizens find that they can make a respectable amount of money simply by participating in the platform, and their enthusiasm for empowr grows even *further*. As more and more people get excited about the platform, they start to bring even greater numbers of their friends on board. This creates an ever-expanding pool of passionate new citizens who are eager to explore every service empowr offers.

While we realize that we can grow our citizen base very quickly through the combination of free membership and an easy learning curve, we also know that is *critically important* for us to create a bulletproof method for helping them monetize their social media activities so that they stay with the platform long term.

Before empowr, social media activities produced revenue for the companies involved but not for users themselves. Because of this, we decided to create a platform that actually compensates citizens who participate actively in the platform (and thus contribute to its success). This seems to be the ideal way to allow our users to leverage skills they already have.

That said, it's all well and good to talk about helping users make money from their everyday social media activities, but actually creating a way to do it was no easy task. The simple answer to the question of how we allow users to monetize their social media participation is this: "With a lot of hard work and a heavy dose of cutting edge technology." But the detailed answer is a bit more interesting.

We can compensate people for using our social platform, even when other platforms can't (or won't), because we've implemented a few key differences in building empowr. First, we generate more revenue per user than any other social network. This is due primarily to our fifteen years (and in my own case, nearly thirty years) of focusing almost exclusively on this challenge. Our combined efforts have resulted in many proprietary and/or patented technologies that help to turn the exchange and sharing of information into revenue.

Second, we are dedicated to keeping costs very low. One of the ways we do this is by crowdsourcing. In the past, due the complexity of the software we were creating, most of our staff worked at our San Diego, California headquarters; but today most of our workforce is located across the globe, working from home.

The third big difference that allows empowr to compensate users for everyday activities is that we spent years focused specifically on the process for delivering compensation to users for posting and sharing content. One of the most complex aspects of empowr, our profit sharing mechanism, took nearly five years of single-minded focus to develop. The process involved seemingly endless hours of trial and error.

To get a sense of the depth and magnitude of the difficulty involved in implementing such a mechanism, consider how easy it would be for a fraudster to use automated software robots (or "bots") to generate fake friends, connections, views—and revenue—for themselves, taking that revenue away from legitimate and honest citizens.

Another way to do this would be with an even worse approach (albeit low-tech) to earning undeserved funds via internet-equipped child sweatshops. These are just a couple of examples of why compensating users for their content views within empowr could never have been accomplished without a significant investment in fraud-busting technology and the know-how needed to properly implement such technology. This type of complex endeavor, given the extremely high likelihood of the project's failure, is outside the patience level and investment horizon of virtually all Silicon Valley venture capitalists and Wall Street investors.

By taking the time to master the process of monetizing social media activity, while also putting in safeguards that protect both the platform and its users from fraud and abuse, we created a highly efficient method of returning the majority of the profits created by empowr to its citizens. This is something that no other business has ever been able to do successfully.

But we didn't stop there. In addition to building a platform that was easy to join and that almost immediately provides new citizens with a small income, we wanted the people who joined empowr to be able to improve their skills continually and to expand their networks so they could earn even more from their work right from the get go.

A Platform That Grows With the Community and Economy

One of the biggest challenges my team and I have faced while creating empowr is linking together an astonishing number of highly complex programs in a way that allows them to work together synergistically. We realized very early on in the platform's development that each piece of the complex software puzzle that is empowr must not only fit together with the other pieces, but it must make the other pieces work even better. *The whole must be greater than the sum of its parts.*

In addition, the structure in which empowr functions must be robust, agile, and dynamic enough to handle explosive growth of our user base and facilitate the billions of financial transactions that such a gargantuan user base will create. And that's just for the software we've created ourselves.

My team and I are also making it very easy for developers to join us and create thousands of other roles for new users to participate in within the platform's economy. As more developers join empowr, the number of products and services we make available to users will increase exponentially each year. In this way, we've ensured that the Network Effect brought on by new, cutting-edge technologies will create new jobs for people, rather than just make old jobs obsolete. The empowr platform has been designed to support a thriving online economy of four billion people.

To run this highly complex economy, and ensure it can adapt to the community's constantly evolving needs and circumstances, we've decided to use the most transparent and reliable government structure ever thought up: *democracy*. From the very first day it opens to the general public, empowr will have a democratically elected company president at its helm. By allowing citizens and employees to vote on different candidates who emerge from the pool of successful citizens within the platform, empowr's structure avoids many of the pitfalls that have forced other companies into stagnation and, ultimately, failure.

As I wrote earlier, companies and countries almost inevitably get fat, dumb, and lazy when one group of top leaders is left in power too long. empowr's democratically elected president will have a single term, which makes it infinitely easier for the platform to continue innovating and changing based on the needs of its citizens. In addition to facilitating innovation, new leadership also prevents people from settling into positions of power within the company for so long that they begin to abuse or neglect their power. Corruption is a word typically associated with the governments of countries, but both intentional corruption and unintentional corruption can be fatal for businesses, as well. This is something I describe in more depth in the chapter that discusses how we approach government.

Having an effective government also means that citizens will be able to ensure that the people running the platform continue to create new opportunities for everyone to succeed and advance within the economy.

Merit-Based Upward Mobility

When people join empowr, we want them to know that they can advance within the platform as far as their work ethic, creativity, and intellect will take them, regardless of how much money they had before they joined. That's why we created a system in which there are a variety of roles that people can grow to fill, regardless of where their particular strengths lie.

A traditional economy relies on people producing, distributing, and/or consuming goods and services. That's why every piece of software that has been integrated into our platform is designed to create innovative new ways for users to produce, distribute, or consume. This is how we ensure that not only are people able to find roles within empowr that they have the skills to fill, but they actually find roles that they *want* to fill.

Another way we make sure that citizens can advance within the platform is by keeping internal advertising as affordable as we can. From the start, we wanted every member of empowr to be able to grow large networks and accelerate their earnings by using advertising products within the platform *without* necessarily paying for them up front.

To do this, we created an advertising system that allows citizens to pay less than 1.5% of the cost of the ads they use each month. Furthermore, this tiny platform fee can be put off until a future date, when citizens look to cash out their earnings. In this way empowr ensures that people who want to work hard to advance within the platform aren't held back by not having a big chunk of money already for investing in their platform activity.

We've managed to keep advertising costs this low by never selling ads to companies who aren't a part of the platform. This may seem counterintuitive, but by restricting the advertising to those users who participate directly in empowr's economy, we've been able to maintain advertising prices that are affordable for nearly all empowr's citizens from the very start of their relationship with us. This approach is one of the key ways in which we ensure upward mobility within the platform while maintaining our focus on poverty-busting.

One other attractive feature of empowr is the opportunity for self-improvement that we offer to our citizens. To make improving skills as appealing as possible, we created a fully integrated educational system for citizens. The boost that empowr's highly effective, low cost (free!) educational system gives to citizens is just one more way that we're ensuring our members are rewarded for their diligence and hard work.

empowr's APPROACH TO EDUCATION

Many educational systems around the world are failing to prepare their students effectively for participation in the modern global economy.

By starting with a small, internal educational system that emphasizes professional teachers, quality-focused recruitment, and high compensation for successful educators, empowr offers a new teaching model that channels the best qualities of some of the world's most successful teaching systems.

Additionally, we leverage technology that incorporates graduate success tracking to offer students a completely transparent view of the value offered by different classes and teachers. This promotes accountability and offers students meaningful choices about which direction to take their education.

In striving to achieve all these goals, our platform uses free-market economic theories to facilitate top-notch, highly productive, student-focused learning.

I've already written about how many educational systems around the world are failing their students. This is a very worrying situation because, every year, in the modern global economy, a solid education becomes more important to the success of individuals and their societies. That's why my team and I have made offering empowr users a highly affordable, efficient educational system one of our highest priorities. To build our own internal educational system, we first researched which national educational systems were most successful on a global scale.

Borrowing from the World's Best Educational Systems

While a large number of nations are struggling to modernize their educational systems, two highly successful countries really stood out in our research: South Korea and Finland. These two countries have very different educational models, but both systems incorporate important concepts that have made them successful. [74] In constructing empowr's educational system, we analyzed which parts of each country's educational system were most conducive to student success.

PISA Rankings by Country and Subject

Mathematics		Reading 55.4%		Science	
Mean score		**Mean score**		**Mean score**	
Shanghai-China	613	Shanghai-China	570	Sanghai-China	580
Singapore	573	Singapore	542	Singapore	551
Chinese Taipei	560	Japan	538	Japan	547
Hong Kong-China	561	Hong Kong-China	545	Finland	545
Korea	554	Korea	536	Hong Kong-China	555
Liechtenstein	535	New Zealand	512	Australia	521
Macao-China	538	Finland	524	New Zealand	516
Japan	536	France	505	Estonia	541
Switzerland	531	Canada	523	Germany	524
Belgium	525	Belgium	509	Netherlands	522
Netherlands	523	Chinese Taipei	523	Korea	538
Germany	514	Australia	512	Canada	525
Poland	518	Ireland	523	United Kingdom	514
Canada	518	Liechtenstein	516	Poland	526
Finland	519	Norway	504	Ireland	522
New Zealand	500	Poland	510	Liechtenstein	525
Australia	504	Netherlands	511	Slovenia	514
Estonia	521	Israel	486	Switzerland	515
Austria	506	Switzerland	509	Belgium	505
Slovenia	501	Germany	508	OECD average	501
Viet Nam	511	Luxembourg	488	Chinese Taipei	523
France	495	United Kingdom	499	Luxembourg	491
Czech Republic	499	OECD average	496	Viet Nam	528
OECD average	494	Estonia	516	France	499
United Kingdom	494	United States	498	Austria	506
Luxembourg	490	Sweden	483	Czech Republic	508
Iceland	493	Macao-China	509	Norway	495
Slovak Republic	482	Italy	490	United States	497
Ireland	501	Czech Republic	493	Denmark	490
Portugal	487	Iceland	483	Macao-China	521
Denmark	500	Portugal	488	Sweden	485
Italy	485	Hungary	488	Italy	494
Norway	489	Spain	488	Hungary	494
Israel	466	Austria	490	Israel	470
Hungary	477	Denmark	496	Iceland	478
United States	481	Greece	477	Lithuania	496

PISA Rankings by Country and Subject[75]

For instance, South Korea's educational system emphasizes hard work and *lots* of studying, and it requires students to be in school almost year-round. Even more important, South Korea's most highly skilled teachers are paid incredibly well (sometimes they become millionaires) and are held accountable through student feedback combined with metrics that track the subsequent success of their own specific students.[76] While this system is *very* stressful for students, the South Korean model of education produces incredibly successful professionals.

Finland, on the other hand, takes a *much* different approach to education by putting much more emphasis on individual attention to students, innovative teaching techniques, and experiential learning. This last component is encouraged by their offering students many hours for extracurricular activities that also include learning opportunities.[77] Also, Finnish teachers are selected from the top 10% of college graduates and are required to obtain a Master's degree in order to get their teaching licenses.[78]

Finally, a large percentage of the Finnish curriculum is comprised of electives, and every student is encouraged to pursue their own passions. The low-stress Finnish educational system produces very healthy and emotionally mature students who also consistently outperform many of their peers in other countries academically.[79]

To create empowr's internal educational system, my team and I took South Korea's teacher compensation and evaluation metrics and combined them with the Finnish system's passion for innovative teaching methods, selective teacher recruitment, and individual student focus. We conducted all this research and focused much of our time on fine-tuning our internal educational system because we recognized from the very beginning of the platform's development process that we were going to have to find really effective ways to help citizens improve their skill sets.

One of the primary reasons that we even created an educational system within empowr was our early realization that a huge percentage of our new citizens would start with only very basic skills. These skills (posting and sharing content) have low economic value—meaning that they contribute very little to the production, distribution, and consumption of goods and services, the three things that are vitally important to any successful economy. Therefore, a critical part of setting up citizens for long-term success is helping users to *improve* their skillsets, by learning from the very most successful educational systems in existence, and then further improving on those lessons through innovation and the use of technology.

Recruiting, Training, and Rewarding High Quality Teachers

To help our citizens gain new skills, we started small by creating an integrated educational system within our own platform. Our online educational system takes the top 10% of our achievers and motivates them to become teachers, known as "success coaches" within our community. We set up our success coaches with excellent trainers who prepare them very well and then we pay our coaches on the same level as the top tenth percentile of all other earners within empowr.

All of our teachers are compensated in a merit-based manner, with no cap on how much a teacher can earn. Additionally, each success coach earns up to 10% of what each of their students earns (at no cost to the student), while being granted the ability to track their students' earnings across all roles within empowr. This, combined with the innate satisfaction many people take in helping others, makes a proven recipe for success.

Our innovative coaching program is also successful in large part because of the powerful social system that the empowr team built into the platform. Bringing billions of people up from zero will require an army of coaches who can give new citizens the personal attention they need to learn new, advanced skills.

The social aspect of the digital economy we've built facilitates this process by pairing less skilled citizens with more skilled citizens. This is done in a way that rewards each person for participating in the process and encourages veteran citizens to take an active role in the growth of empowr by becoming coaches for new citizens.

Another critically important piece of our coaching program is that, over many years, we have carefully watched what our most successful coaches have done in their day-to-day activities and have automated much of that work for them, taking the most repetitive tasks out of their daily to-do lists. As a result, this has freed up all our coaches to find new and innovative ways to teach their students how to succeed. Coaches have a great deal of freedom in determining how they teach, what their schedule is, and how they convey information to their students (to name just a few examples of the flexibility they are given). By doing this, empowr creates an environment in which educators *also* become innovators who can explore new teaching frontiers.

Using Free-Market Economics, Transparency, and Accountability to Improve Teaching

With new ideas, there is always a chance of failure. And while we do everything we can to give our coaches the tools and support they need to succeed, it's also important to allow unsuccessful ideas to fail. If coaches try new teaching programs or techniques that students review negatively or that fail to produce students who go on to find success, fewer students will be willing to learn from them and, eventually, the less effective instructors and classes will course-correct or be weeded out.

The good classes and coaches are separated from the ineffective through the use of very basic free-market economics. Supply and demand dictates the value of products and services, so if a coach is good at her job and she produces satisfied, successful graduates, more students will want to learn from her, and the demand for her services will go up. On the other hand, when a coach is ineffective at her job and her graduates fail to find success, fewer students will want to work with her, and the demand for her services will go down.

This highly functional free-market educational model is made possible because, from the customers' perspective, we provide unprecedented transparency. We do this by allowing them to see a variety of metrics on their potential coaches. These metrics give students educational choices and even further increase their chances of succeeding. The metrics track a variety of things, including analyzing the success of each coach's previous students by measuring students' income after they have received instruction from a given teacher. Other metrics show the responsiveness and availability—calculated by the platform—and the rating of each coach (provided by their former students).

Another factor that contributes to the success of our free-market education model is the high availability of coaches. One of the most encouraging things we've learned since creating empowr is that people *love* teaching others to succeed, so it made perfect sense for us to leverage our technology in a way that rewards them for doing so.

The coaching aspect of our educational system is successful in large part because Facebook, Twitter and other social media platforms have done an incredible job of training over a billion people to use their platforms. As mentioned earlier, our user interface has been designed to look as familiar as possible. This means that, right out of the gate, we have a minimum of one billion potential users who can slip easily into basic coaching roles or other community positions. Since there's no cost to participate, this means our pool of potential coaches is nearly unlimited.

By holding our success coaches accountable for the quality of their teaching, by compensating them without any caps or limits, and by offering students a meaningful choice in the direction they elect to take their education, empowr offers students unprecedented control over their professional growth.

Why Our Educational Model is Better than Others

In recent years there has been an explosion of new online teaching models. These experimental educational platforms have stirred a highly productive debate about the future of education, and how it fits into the evolving post-industrial global economy. As a result of this rich debate, many new online platforms have been created that offer students access to an unprecedented array of classes and teachers. From learning how to write code to taking free online history classes at Ivy League universities, the new frontier of education has most definitely moved to the Internet.

One very popular online educational system that has done a wonderful job in expanding the frontiers of modern education is the Khan Academy. The brilliant founder of the academy, Salman Khan, started out by using the Internet to tutor some of his relatives. When members of his extended family found out how valuable his instruction was, they also asked him to tutor them. Eventually Mr. Khan was inundated with requests from people eager to benefit from his intellectual generosity.

Once he found how hungry so many people were to learn new things, Mr. Khan expanded his teaching and began offering even more programs to students around the world. While the Academy has faced some relatively mild criticism in the past, there can be no doubt that it has had a very positive effect on the world and on teaching, in general, by demonstrating how successful, effective, and popular an online teaching institution can be.

That said, there are still a lot of problems with the new online teaching platforms. For one, the most recent tech-based approaches to teaching don't put any real emphasis on turning teaching into the top profession that it deserves to be. For example, few platforms motivate teachers to fully dedicate their time to teaching by paying them what they are really worth.

Top-notch teachers provide an *incredible* value to their students and to society in general. There would be many more great teachers if they were compensated according to the phenomenal value they add to the world. As Microsoft's Bill Gates has observed, "Research shows that there is only half as much variation in student achievement between schools as there is among classrooms in the same school. If you want your child to get the best education possible, it is actually more important to get him assigned to a *great teacher* than to a great school."[80]

In addition to issues with proper teacher compensation and professionalization, none of the new online platforms offer students the opportunity to assess the value of the courses being offered objectively and comprehensively. This situation has resulted in students having a million different choices when it comes to pursuing their online education but very few options for calculating the value of the courses.

Mastering new skills can be time-consuming, so this scenario leaves many students frustrated because they aren't able to determine which educational choices will provide them with the most "bang for their buck."

It's for all these reasons that empowr's teaching model is better for students. By selecting our success coaches from the best and brightest within our community, by training them well and giving them the high levels of compensation required to attract, retain, and focus the very best our economy has to offer, we provide students with access to incredibly skilled educators. On top of that, we provide all potential students with access to real-time statistics and metrics that show the ability (or inability) of our coaches to prepare their students for future success.

It's this last part—the rich integration of our educational software into every aspect of our economy—that I believe *really* sets our educational system apart from others. Because of the many earning roles that people can fill within empowr, we are able to track internally how much each student's income improves once they graduate from different coaches' programs and thus analyze exactly how well each teacher prepares his or her students to participate in the platform's economy. By providing potential students with simple access to these analyses, we enable them to make smart, informed decisions about their educational future before they invest any of their valuable time into their education.

Even if other educational systems do manage to achieve the levels of transparency that empowr provides, without the *ability to track the success levels* of all students comprehensively after they graduate and to *allow students to view that data* literally on the same web page where they choose their teachers, that transparency will be of less value to their students—and so, in those educational systems, the true free-market dynamics that is so badly needed will continue to be a fantasy. Not until we are fully able to treat education like any other product—allowing incentives, competition, and customer choice to determine the winners and losers—will students get the high quality education that they, their time, their money, and their societies deserve.

Improving Education Also Improves Democracy

While our internal educational system is now relatively small, my team and I believe that, as it produces more and more successful graduates, we will be able to expand it every year. Eventually, our goal is to provide comprehensive educational choices within our online community that prepare students to succeed within empowr, while also offering them intellectual enrichment that allows them to participate more effectively in the platform's governance.

Because education is such an important part of a successful economy, by providing citizens with access to a comprehensive educational system that works well, empowr will enhance every aspect of its existence. Better education will lead to even more effective company officials and presidents with every election cycle and eventually will allow the platform to run more efficiently than nearly any other company or country.

By offering citizens many different ways to lift themselves out of poverty based on skills they already have and by giving them free access to an educational system that allows them to improve their skills and hone their minds, we will enable people to create a top-notch government to run every aspect of our business. It's our belief that effective governance is critical to the success of any organization, and that's why we've put so much thought and software into how empowr is run.

empowr's APPROACH TO GOVERNMENT

Large organizations function best when the people in charge are accountable to those they govern; hence, democracy is the best system of government.

Since empowr aims to be the world's first successful Democratic Social Economy, we must put together the best version of democracy we can possibly create. By gathering the best minds from around the world to create a democratic form of corporate governance that learns from the mistakes of the world's other democracies, empowr aims to create an exemplary online model of democracy that makes users crave effective national democratic governance.

In doing so, my team and I believe our democratic corporation or "Demporation" will play a small role in helping spread responsible, transparent, democratic governance across the globe while also encouraging many existing democratic governments to step up their game.

Amartya Sen, winner of the 1998 Nobel Peace Prize in Economics once wrote, "A country does not have to be deemed fit for democracy; rather, it has become fit through democracy." Indeed, since its inception and throughout humanity's history, democracy has improved the lots of billions of people across our world by increasing economic prosperity and making the people who govern countries more accountable to their societies.

empowr will channel the power of democracy into governing our organization in a way that creates profits while it also represents the values and interests of the employees and citizens who make the platform so successful. In this way, the company will, as Amartya says, become even more fit through democracy.

With that goal in mind, it's important to analyze how and why some existing democracies function well versus other democracies that are having trouble. To do this, my team and I are bringing in some of the sharpest experts on national democratic governance to help us build our own corporate government, by creating a genuinely democratic—inclusive and participatory—crowdsourced constitutional process. Some of the brightest minds from around the world are contributing to the project, and, when we're finished, we'll have created democracy 3.0. As Yale Professor of Political Science Hélène Landemore noted, "*Democracy 1.0* was Ancient Greece. 18th century democracies—representative governments as we still know them—defined *Democracy 2.0*. What empowr is doing is a break from Democracy 2.0 because it's online, global, and goes way beyond our trite conception of political institutions. So this is Democracy 3.0. empowr is revolutionizing a 2,500 year history."

Learning from the Mistakes of Troubled Democracies

So, what are some of the lessons we've already learned from other democracies that will help empowr run its own government?

First, *top political positions must be limited to those with substantial records of having successfully served the public.* One of the most disappointing aspects of some modern democracies is that there many people elected to high office who have very little business being there. This is largely because of the increasingly powerful influence that big money has on modern politics and on candidates, themselves. As a result of this influence, there has been a lot less emphasis on whether the candidates have a record of successfully serving in public office.

In the context of empowr's government, this means that only candidates who have a history of being effective success coaches will be allowed to run for political office within the corporation. This makes it much less likely that people running for office will be unprepared for the demands of the offices they intend to fill. Another benefit is that, by limiting the candidate pool to those who have served as success coaches within the platform, we give voters a chance to make an apples-to-apples comparison of how good each candidate has been at their job—i.e., improving the lives of the people they represented—in the past.

This process ensures that when voters consider the ideas that candidates talk about during their campaigns for office, they can bear in mind how successfully those candidates have implemented other ideas in the past. It's nice for politicians to be able to "talk the talk," but being able to look at (and quantifiably compare) their records and see if they can actually "walk the walk" is even more valuable. By setting our political system up this way, we force candidates to run on their record so that they must not only give themselves credit for past successes but also hold themselves accountable for previous failures.

The second thing we've learned from other democracies is that the *most successful politicians are those who are more concerned with effectively governing than with being reelected.* When politicians stay in power too long, they often get far too comfortable with their jobs in a way that reduces government efficiency.

As elected officials remain in office for extended periods of time, they develop cozy relationships with other people in power, and, eventually, even the most upstanding politicians often succumb to some form of corruption. Sometimes the corruption takes a softer, *unintentional* shape, where people and companies are given preferential treatment because they have been effective in the past. Other times, the corruption takes on a more insidious form, and politicians simply start taking bribes or begin to peddle their influence.

One way to avoid this type of scenario is by only allowing elected officials to hold office for one term. This makes certain that after they are elected, politicians will only be concerned with doing the best job they can for the duration of their term. By ensuring that new, passionate leaders are always at the helm, this system encourages innovation and adaptation to new challenges as they arise. That's why empowr's democratically elected president is only allowed to serve one term and is never permitted to run for reelection.

The third lesson we've learned from other democracies is that *government programs that distribute taxpayer money to specific groups within the nation must have expiration dates.* If government money is used to give businesses or individuals a leg up for too long, the money is eventually used to influence government in an increasingly negative way.

One instance of this occurring here in the United States is with farm subsidies. In the past, subsidies were offered to independent farmers in order to help maintain the prices of basic staple goods that millions of Americans relied upon to live. The government gave each farmer a certain amount of money to produce a certain crop; this ensured that the cost of basic foodstuffs remained predictable.

What has happened in the years since the program was created is that many small farms have been bought up by huge, multinational corporations that generate billions of dollars in profits each year. Despite this huge change in the dynamics of American farming, the U.S. government continues to spend billions of dollars on subsidies which are given primarily to huge, already profitable businesses.

These big businesses, in turn, use a portion of their government subsidies to lobby politicians to keep the "government cheese" coming each year. As a result, billions of taxpayer dollars are thrown away each year, millions of tons of food are wasted, and thousands of acres of farmland are not used efficiently. Needless to say, this is not an ideal situation.

To avoid this mistake within empowr, every aspect of the business on which we spend a significant amount of revenue will be subject to a transparent, comprehensive bi-yearly renewal process. If the company intends to continue spending money on anything, it needs to start anew the process of "getting permission" from its elected officials and citizens every two years. In this way, our business will ensure that wasteful spending is much more limited. By properly administering corporate spending, we'll ensure that revenue is either given to the citizens through our profit-sharing mechanisms or spent on effective, results-driven projects that improve the platform and its overall performance.

While the process is still ongoing, we've already combined all of these lessons into our business model of a **dem**ocratically governed cor**poration**, which we call a *"Demporation."*

Creating the World's First Demporation

Another famous quote about democracy comes from Winston Churchill, in a speech he gave to the British House of Commons following the Second World War. Churchill said, "It has been said that democracy is the worst form of government except all those other forms that have been tried from time to time." While the purpose of this quote was obviously to get a bit of a laugh, it also eloquently points out that other systems of governance have been tried, and they've all been pretty awful.

Possibly the most unique aspect of empowr is the fact that the citizens have a direct say over who runs the company. Most big companies today are controlled by a board of directors whose only real goal is to make shareholders as much money as possible and who are often entrenched in a way that makes them highly unresponsive to customers. This leads to a huge degree of inertia in the way many businesses are run, which damages them and makes them much less competitive.

As mentioned above, empowr avoids this inertia because the company is run by a president who has in mind not only the interests of the shareholders but also those of the citizens (customers and the employees). This is facilitated through a regular election in which citizens elect the company's president. The election is transparent and fair, in that all the candidates are given access to the same resources and subjected to the same level of scrutiny. By participating in this election, citizens can influence the development and growth of the business in much the same way that, in an ideal world, citizen voters influence national democracies.

By giving the people who are most critical to the business's success a powerful voice in how the business evolves, empowr engages customers and employees at a level that has been previously unheard of. This engagement, combined with the highly competitive election process, means that only the best of the best are elected to run the business and that all the people who are most important to a business feel personally accountable for its success.

This isn't to say that we're creating a charity or setting up a giant drum circle where we can all sing *Kumbaya*. Free-market capitalism is an integral part of why the new Demporation model that empowr runs on will turn out to be vastly more profitable than the traditional corporate structure. Businesses already understand that engaged customers and employees are critical to a company's success, because, if these two groups are properly engaged with a company, it will result in a huge positive difference in the company's bottom line. Businesses have also realized that product development via customer centricity improves their bottom line as well.

Bearing all this in mind, empowr is structured in a way that gives a large degree of control to its customers at the highest levels of the company with the specific intent of engaging them with the business. By engaging customers, the business model is also designed to maximize customer centricity. By successfully leveraging these two important drivers, empowr should end up being very successful.

When other large businesses notice how profitable the Demporation model can be, it's almost a given that there will eventually be a strong push from shareholders to adopt it before their competitors do (or as a result of their competitors doing so).

There exist significant impediments for a corporation that wants to transform itself into a Demporation, however. Some of those obstacles are know-how related, and others are more technical in nature. Companies will need to figure out how to run an election with their customers; which includes how to block fraudulent votes to ensure the voting process remains legitimate. They'll need to figure out what steps or stages are needed for the transformation, along with the optimal path and timing for the move to becoming a Demporation—so as to near-eliminate the risk of something going sideways during the process that could distract management or damage the company's momentum, revenues or reputation.

At empowr, we believe if more and more corporations become Demporations, one major and positive side-effect for society will be that everyday people will gain more influence in politics, through those corporate vehicles, since those same corporations have today become quite powerful in democracies. By voting for the President of the company, people can influence who runs the company; so if one candidate running to be the company's president promises movement on, say, the company's impact on the environment or its government lobbying efforts on another issue, by voting for her instead of her competitors, people will now have gained influence in those areas.

As discussed, when everyday people gain more influence in their democracies, democracies work better—and helping to return influence to people in democracies is part of empowr's stated mission: "Empowering people by enabling opportunity, hope and influence."

Therefore, in order to help corporations overcome challenges to becoming Demporations, we plan on providing to them our know-how and technologies, gained over years of trial and error.

Rather than take more space and time here to discuss the merits of Demporations and how I believe they will transform countries and politics, the relationship between labor and capital, and societies as a whole, I am authoring a separate book that focuses on that singular topic, which I won't publish until empowr has succeeded to a sufficient enough level such that it can be modeled scientifically as a working proof of concept. Dozens of economists and political scientists, mostly from academia, have joined us in this effort, to ensure the process we've undertaken is documented in accordance with rigid scientific methodology.

As a consequence of becoming Demporations, corporations will of course become more responsive to the needs of their customers and employees. While this is a fantastic side effect of what my team and I are creating, it's my hope that our positive influence on governance won't stop with just businesses.

Lately, democracy has come under attack across the globe. I believe this is primarily because many democracies have allowed themselves to become too top heavy and have lost their focus on providing for the needs of their people. I believe it's time to *bring honor back to politics* and *return power to the people* who are crying out for better governance across the planet.

As empowr grows and millions of people around the world join, the positive effects of a well-run democracy will become better and better known each year. When enough people begin to take notice of how well empowr is running and, as a result, how much it's improving their lives, governments will start taking notice as well.

Eventually, as empowr grows and starts to have a bigger influence on people's lives as well as on the global economy, I hope some of the reforms that we've built into our democracy

2.0 model will become more appealing to voters and to national governments. In this way, everybody at empowr is working toward playing our part in delivering an online democracy that will make a contribution to improving national democracies.

CONCLUSION

The world is full of powerful technologies and ideas that can be leveraged to help address humanity's most daunting problems. The key to doing this is examining carefully which problems are putting our planet in the most danger and which factors are most important to humanity's success.

Democratic governance, education, and network technology are three forces that can be molded into powerful tools for the advancement of our species. By building a business specifically dedicated to refining these tools in ways that contribute to solving our biggest problems, empowr's real goal is to improve the quality of life of every person our platform touches.

We hope you've enjoyed the book, and that perhaps you've even become passionate about our mission. There are many ways to join us and many ways to compete with us. Whatever you decide to do we wish you luck and look forward to getting to know you.

" Shoot for the moon. Even if you miss, you'll land among the stars." These inspiring words from motivational speaker Les Brown quite effectively summarize a core philosophical precept to which my team and I subscribe. Another way to think about how we approach the mission we've undertaken is, "Where there is a will, there is a way." Basically, if we didn't believe so powerfully in what we are doing, there's no way we'd be able even to attempt to take on some of the humongous global problems we've set out to address.

So, bearing all those ideals in mind, what exactly has this book been all about?

The Big Problems

We live in a world where some of the most potent global forces for positive change are slowly being subverted to serve smaller subsets of the world's population. If this situation continues to get worse each year, it will inevitably contribute further to a world where a small portion of humanity lives in the lap of luxury while the majority of people fight for the table scraps *or* it will lead to a global conflict that will dwarf all the other conflicts humanity has ever witnessed.

Democracy, often written about as a shining beacon of governance that ensures even the most downtrodden members of society still have a voice, has been almost entirely hijacked by big money and special interests. As giant corporations and the new global elite continue to entrench their control of national governance and of the world's economic infrastructure, huge swaths of humanity become further and further disenfranchised.

Despite a shocking level of dissatisfaction with the way their countries are being run, average voters seem powerless to change the course of the behemoth vessels of civilization on which we are all passengers. As countries that were once paragons of democracy slowly slip into oligarchy or something even worse, global enthusiasm for democracy is waning.

Education, the driving power behind every major technological revolution and intellectual advancement, is being neglected and left to stagnate, even as its importance to both individual and national success becomes more vital with each passing year. Many institutions of higher learning that were once the gold standard of intellectual enrichment have slowly been converted into rubber stamp factories that do nothing more than allow people to put meaningless letters on their resumes.

Organizations, economies, and the world in general are growing in complexity each year. Even as this trend accelerates, the educational systems that should be helping people understand the world in which they live instead are being held captive by broken bureaucracy and politics, while they slowly wind their way toward obsolescence.

Network technology, once held up as the key to a prosperous future for the entire human race, is quietly being monopolized by a few terrifyingly entities that are set up only to concern themselves with profits. Few of the people within the entities pushing toward this monopolization fully comprehend the shortsighted nature of their efforts and the perilous path on which their choices are putting our species, or are in a position to change that path.

As network technologies and the machines they connect become exponentially more capable with each generation, eating up the jobs that helped workers feed their families, the few alarms being raised by the scientists and engineers responsible for such high-tech wonders are being silenced by the mountains of wealth that their supposed genius generates. The long-term threat of their technological offspring is obscured by the temporary benefits created by each new iteration of machine and software.

As they are left unaddressed, all of these very serious global problems contribute to world poverty and inequality more and more each year. Time and again throughout our history, when we don't give people the tools to understand their world and move it forward by peacefully changing it for the better, they soon become vulnerable to sinister ideologies and charismatic manipulators who eventually care only for power.

This, in turn, creates breeding grounds for extremists, terrorists, and dictators who ultimately end up creating even more poverty and inequality. As these societal viruses work their way through the regions that host them, they eventually spread and infect the global body. The more interconnected our world becomes, the more the suffering of the few can hurt the lives of the many.

So, what can we do about all this nastiness?

The Solutions

American General Creighton Abrams once said, "When eating an elephant, take one bite at a time." And to be sure, each of the big problems mentioned above is an elephant in its own right. Therefore, the only way to deal with these gigantic global challenges is to chip away at them piece by piece. That's why our strategy focuses *on rediscovering and enhancing the good side of each of the powerful forces* that have been commandeered, and *on refocusing those forces* on the task for which they were originally created: **making the world a better place for everybody.**

Democracy is more than just a word; it's the idea that the people who make an organization successful should, in turn, be taken care by that organization when it succeeds. On a global level, this means that the wellbeing of the lower and middle classes, whose hard work and sacrifice create the opportunities for their countries to thrive, should be a high priority for the people running each country's government. Only by ensuring that upward social mobility is measurable and real will the lower and middle classes remain motivated, focused, and productive in societies.

empowr allows people to see how successful a large, democratically run organization can be if its governance is structured in a way that emphasizes some of the best things about democracy: passionate, responsive leaders with new ideas focused on the good of the whole that also protect individual liberties; and a transparent, accountable government that quickly adapts to address new problems.

By building the world's first democratic technology corporation and by delivering successful, practical democracy over the Internet to millions of people around the world, we hope to rekindle a global passion for democracy that we believe will make at least a small contribution to creating new democracies while also improve the ones that already exist.

Education is one of the most important drivers of a successful, modern society, and the *people* who are most important to education are teachers. That means that, in order to have a top-notch educational system, societies must produce talented teachers and give them the tools, freedoms, and compensation they require to do their jobs effectively.

In addition to creating great teachers, an educational system must be transparent, responsive and accountable, and offer students an effective way to plan their academic careers. To do this, the system should focus on teaching students highly marketable skills and the ability to think critically, while also provide them with an effective way to compare classes and teachers so they can make informed decisions about which courses to take.

empowr does this already on a small scale with our internal educational system, and, as we grow, our education system will grow with us. Eventually, along with providing students with transparency and accountability that enable everyone to evaluate both teachers and the courses they offer comprehensively, we'll offer a huge variety of educational choices. Doing this will not only make our citizens' skills more valuable but will help them to expand their minds in ways that make them more effective democratic participants.

Network technology and the Network Effect it creates do not have to be blights on humanity. Rather than destroy jobs and concentrate wealth in the hands of a few powerful organizations and individuals, network technology can instead be a force for good. But before this can be done, an organization must commit to figuring out how to leverage the Network Effect in a way that focuses on uplifting all the people it touches. It just so happens that that empowr *is* that organization.

Each of empowr's strategies has been designed from the ground up to *benefit from being networked*. As more people get involved in each component of our platform, they increase the value of the network that they participate in exponentially. Our political system will improve as more people join, bringing new ideas and passion to what we do. Our educational system will become more sophisticated every year, as new, highly intelligent people come on board and add their own innovative ideas to the mix.

As the value of each component of empowr grows exponentially thanks to the Network Effect and the sophisticated technologies our engineers have developed, our company will be able to return even more money to the citizens who make the platform succeed. Additionally, the success of each part of empowr will enhance the positive impact every other part of the platform has on the community. As our revenues grow, our platform will increase in size and efficiency until *billions* of people around the planet benefit every day from their participation.

The more people who join, the more empowr can do to show people how to lift themselves out of poverty and become increasingly effective global citizens. The final result is a world where people have many different choices about which direction to take their lives and what education is required to think critically about the ideas they encounter every day.

In this best-case scenario, the people who once would have been easy targets for power-hungry charlatans, terrorists, and extremists are equipped with the financial and intellectual tools they need to tell all those blighters where to shove it. Thus, rather than become petri dishes for some of the worst aspects of our modern world, poor countries and regions instead become engines of hope and positive change.

The American Dream

The American Dream is a term that attempts to describe a set of ideals based on freedom, which include the opportunities for achievement, affluence, and an upward social mobility for anyone who is willing to work hard in a society with few artificial barriers, including restrictions that limit people based on their social class, ethnicity, religion, or race. In the definition of the American Dream by James Truslow Adams in 1931, "life should be better and richer and fuller for everyone, with opportunity for each according to ability or achievement" regardless of social class or circumstances of birth.[81]

The American Dream and the simpler and singular word, *America*—these are both *ideas*; concepts that resonate with emotion for people everywhere in the world. Who doesn't want a better life for themselves and their loved ones?

However, much like a gorgeous flower garden that requires constant weed pulling and efforts to stay beautiful, the last few decades have taught us that the American Dream, personal freedom, and democracy won't automatically endure without constant effort and a willingness to fight to get them back on track... not in America nor anywhere else in the world.

As a result of reading this book, my hope is that you now see that the fight is a critically important one, that it desperately needs you, and that joining empowr is one path to joining that fight.

◆◆◆

So, how do you become a part of empowr?

Joining empowr and Fighting the Good Fight

On empowr, there are many different ways to join the fight as a member of a community that's working on global solutions to some of the world's biggest problems. You can quickly sign up as a citizen and explore the community yourself. Come and participate in some of the interesting discussions and provocative debates that take place every day. Invite your friends on board and interact with them while also creating a bit of revenue for yourself.

Soon afterwards, as you get more familiar with the platform and all that it offers, maybe you'll want to become a success coach. By mentoring new citizens and showing them how to get the most out of their experience with empowr, you'll probably grow even more enthusiastic about what you're doing and about the whole platform, in general. By being part of our success coach program, you'll get to try new and innovative ways to teach your students and find satisfaction by providing passionate, motivated people with tools to improve their lives.

Perhaps after you've established a winning track record as a success coach, you'll decide to join the ranks of empowr's politicians. You might run for office in empowr on a campaign platform that advocates for fantastic new ideas that my team and I have never even thought of. Once you're elected, you'll be able to try these new ideas out and see how your hard work, dedication, and commitment can reach across the world to help foster good.

Or maybe you'd like to join the team at our offices in San Diego, California? We're always looking for talented software engineers, analysts, designers, business development and product managers, among other roles. Now that you know what we're trying to do and why, if you're ready to move to sunny San Diego, drop me a line here: JoinTheTeam@empowr.com. I promise I'll get back to you personally. You can also learn more about our career opportunities here: empowr.com/Careers.

Or, maybe you want to build a platform that's better than empowr?

Competing With empowr or Following a Different Path

Since the very beginning of this book, I've said that competition is one of the biggest drivers of successful organizations. I don't think empowr is any different. If you've read this book and you genuinely believe that you have better ideas about how to leverage the technology my team and I have created to do some good then please let us know.

At empowr, we feel that the success or failure of a technology should be judged not by the number of products it manufactures or the number of services it provides but by the number of lives it improves and the degree to which it improves them.

My team and I all care *far* more about the long-term effects of what we're creating here at empowr than the short-term monetary benefits we get. We really hope to create new global opportunities for humanity to *do* better and to *be* better. If that means sharing our business model secrets and our technologies with other businesses and individuals who can do a more effective job of building those global opportunities, then so be it.

I hope very much that you've enjoyed reading this book. My team and I wish you all the best in whatever you choose to do with your life. Whether you decide to join us, compete with us, or have nothing whatsoever to do with us, may good fortune accompany you wherever your journey takes you.

ACKNOWLEDGMENTS

Writing a book while holding down a full-time job requires a lot of help, and I received a lot of it from some wonderful people. For starters, from my mom and dad, as well as from Jasmin, Sky, and Sydney, without whose ongoing love, lessons, support, sacrifices, and forgiveness this project or book would never have been attempted.

I thank my remarkable co-founder and BFF, Brandie Lee Smith, without whose nearly two decades of double full-time dedication, optimism, and belief in me the entire empowr project would not have started or survived.

I thank my other co-founders including the resourceful Trupti Patel for keeping the lights on for the last decade; how she did it, I will never quite understand. The meticulous Mohit Vazirani for keeping the data intact, safe, and accessible for nearly ten years, despite a total lack of resources. The ingenious Christopher Lee for keeping all the code moving forward and in his head during that same decade; how that head didn't explode I still don't know. The unrelenting Scott Garcia for helping me build the business logic and moving the product and technical operations forward for the majority of the last decade. The steady Ashley Woodward for her grace under pressure year after year; and the assertive and masterful Bryan Wilson for his continued and growing engineering leadership, expertise, and WTAWTAW. There exist a number of other heroes—too many to list here—but these folks represent the others quite well, none of whom ever wanted or asked for recognition. All but one of these amazing warriors have given this mission and gargantuan effort the majority of their adult years, staying focused and walking away from significant opportunities in order to ensure empowr would continue marching forward. Without their sacrifice, neither empowr nor this book would have been possible.

empowr's first democratically-elected President and master juggler Brian Woosley, voted into the company by the citizens, has been *the* warrior for this book, most responsible for helping me bring all the required pieces together. Thank you, Brian, thank you Gary Scott and Kathryn Galán for your professionalism and editing with a smile.

To my friends and former colleagues that keep reminding me that I am forgiven for disappearing from the face of the planet in order to give everything I have to this project and, more recently, this book: That means a lot to me. I miss you, and I thank you for always cheering me on from the sidelines and being there for me.

I am grateful to the thousands of employees who gave parts of their lives by joining me on this journey through one or more of the companies leading up to empowr, especially collegeclub.com, along with the many companies it acquired along its path including CollegeStudent.com, Versity.com, eStudentLoan.com, Campus24.com and CollegeBeat.com; without the learnings gained from those projects via your sacrifices, empowr would not exist today. And neither would Facebook, which only rose up from the dot-com market and collegeclub's ashes after you successfully cleared the market of dozens of well-funded college competitors to create the perfect vacuum in that most coveted of spaces.

And finally, a giant Thank You to the alpha users and success coaches that gave freely of their time and lives to this project. I am humbled by how much you gave and continue to give to this mission. I look forward to meeting you sometime in the coming months or years, to shake your hands and break bread—and learn your personal story and reasons behind your willingness to give so much to this project and mission.

ABOUT THE AUTHOR

Michael C. Pousti founded his first start-up while still a computer engineering student at UC San Diego in his senior year. Employing 200 people and generating millions of dollars in profits by the age of twenty-two, his company Higher Educational Resources Corp. developed the first commercially successful search engine on the Internet—then still called the Arpanet.

After his next start-up, Productivity Solutions Corporation, was acquired when he was twenty-four, Mike decided he was done with the corporate world and returned to UCSD to study psychology.

Inspired by his class work (specifically, Abraham Maslow's conclusions around the innate need for purpose), at age twenty-six he started CollegeClub.com with aspirations of bringing accountability to higher education. With the help of partnerships with NBC Universal, Sony Corporation, General Motors, and Ericsson, CollegeClub.com became the world's #1 website for the 18-23 year old demographic.

CollegeClub.com filed an S1 with the SEC for an initial public offering (IPO) in early 2000, only to have the Nasdaq plunge and dot-com crash cause virtually all IPOs to be blocked for the next few years. CollegeClub.com was acquired, and less than a week later, Pousti and his co-founder Brandie Smith started phase 1 of empowr.

During their research for empowr, Pousti and Smith discovered and documented a two-way relationship between democracy and poverty in countries, where poverty caused democracies to fail; and a lack of democracy created poverty. As a result, they set out to build and deliver, using the Internet, a combined economy and democracy—or "Democratic Social Economy."

empowr's stated goal is to help four billion people earn an average of $25 USD/day by the year 2025. To meet that goal, it has successfully resisted the lure of Wall Street banks and Silicon Valley venture capitalists so that the company and its profits can belong solely to the platform's citizens and employees.

Inspired by the project's social objectives and audacious goal, over 1,000 product and engineering professionals left companies like Yahoo, Microsoft, Price Waterhouse, Genentech and Google to join Pousti—for little or no pay—at the San Diego, California-based research facility, where Pousti had meticulously architected a unique corporate culture in order to foster innovation at unprecedented levels.

Hundreds of inventions resulted, and the highly patented suite of technologies generated over $150M U.S. for empowr, allowing the company to self-fund and stay true to its original goal and approach. Today, empowr's proprietary technologies are utilized by all major social platforms including Facebook, Twitter, Instagram, Google Plus and Tumblr. For a list of many of those inventions, visit www.Google.com/Patents and enter *Pousti* into the search field.

In accordance with the democratic ideals of empowr, Pousti, and his co-founder Brandie Smith, recently relinquished their CEO and President positions, respectively. They handed over control of the company to empowr's citizens, who formally elected their leader (and new President of empowr) via a web-based election.

Later this year (2015), the effort to crowdsource, draft and ratify the empowr constitution will be led by Yale University in cooperation with nearly 100 political scientists and economists from industry and universities such as Harvard, M.I.T., Stanford, UC Berkeley and Duke University.

No longer a full-time employee, Pousti continues to serve empowr as a member of empowr's board of directors.

ABOUT empowr

empowr is an experiment—a partnership between academia and tech entrepreneurs that's attempting to deliver a democratized social media experience where the company is governed by its citizens.

The company's patented platform aims to provide economic opportunities for its citizens and return virtually all of the company revenues to them. empowr achieves this by democratizing the core elements of social media, including user interface/design, advertising and marketplace platforms, as well as the company's governance, leadership and profits.

After years of research, development and testing with 100,000 citizens in its "closed alpha" phase, at the time of this writing in late 2015, empowr is in the final stages of preparation to reopen the platform to the world as part of its "open alpha" stage.

For more on empowr, visit www.empowr.com.

REFERENCES

[1]Madslien, Jorn. "Dot Com Bubble Burst: 10 Years On." *http://new.bbc.co.uk.* 9 March 2010.

[2] "J7: The July 7 Truth Campaign." julyseventh.co.uk.

[3] The Editors of Encyclopedia Britannica. "Konrad Adenauer, Chancellor of West Germany." *www.britannica.com.* Last updated 28 May 2015.

[4] Henderson, David R. "German Economic Miracle." *The Concise Encyclopedia of Economics, 2nd edition.*

[5] Gaddis, John Lewis. *The Cold War: A New History.* New York: Penguin, 2005.

[6] Morwean. "Occupied Berlin." *Wikimedia Creative Commons.* "File:Occupiedberlin.png," recolored, retitled. 8 Dec 2014.

[7] History.com staff. "Berlin Airlift." *A&E Networks.* 2011.

[8] Lahmeyer, Jon. "Statistisches Jahrbuch der Deutschen Demokratischen Republik." *www.Populstat.info/Euro/germanec.* 10 Feb 2002.

[9] McDonald, Lachie. "2012: Time Out—Berlin." *LachieTravel. blogspot.* 23 Oct 2012.

[10] History.com staff. "Berlin Airlift." *A&E Networks.* 2011.

[11] Hanson, Phillip. *The Rise and Fall of the Soviet Economy: An Economic History of the USSR from 1945.* Essex, England: Longman/Pearson Education, Ltd., 2003

[12] Swindell, Gary S. "World Oil & Natural Gas Statistics and Graphs." *GSwindell.com.* Oct 2010.

[13] Barro, Josh. "95% of Income Gains Since 2009 Went to the Top 1%—Here's What that Really Means." *Business Insider.* 12 Sep 2013.

[14] Walmsley, Roy. "World Prison Population List (tenth edition)." *International Centre for Prison Studies.* 21 Nov 2013.

[15] "Annual Inflation Rate in the United States from 1990 to 2014." www.*Statista.com.* Jan 2015.

[16] "Bridging the Gap." *The Economist.* 28 June 2015. Print Edition.

[17] Abelson, Reed. "While the U.S. Spends Heavily on Health Care, a Study Faults the Quality." *The New York Times.* 17 July 2008.

[18] "Congress and the Public." *Gallup.com.* © 2015.

[19] Glassman, Matthew Eric. "Congressional Careers: Service Tenure and Patterns of Member Service, 1789-2015." *Congressional Research Service.* 3 Jan 2015.

[20] Sorokina, Marina. "Between Faith and Reason: Waldemar Haffkine (1860-1930) in India." In: *Western Jews in India: From the Fifteenth Century to the Present.* Wenneth X. Robbins and Marvin Tokayer, ed.s. Delhi: Manohar: 2013. 161-178

[21] "Cholera's Seven Pandemics." *CBC/Radio-Canada News.* 9 May 2008/22 Oct 2010.

[22] Bolton, J. L. "Looking for *Yersinia pestis*: Scientists, Historians and the Black Death" in: *The Fifteenth Century XII: Society in an Age of Plague.* Linda Clark and Carole Rawcliffe, eds. Woodbridge, England: Boydell Press, 2013. 15.

[23] Oshinsky, David M. *Polio: An American Story.* Oxford: Oxford University Press, 2006.

[24] Deciutiis, Hanna Jane. "Bill Gates Weighs In on Higher Education, Newspapers in Interview with *The Daily Texan." The Daily Texan.* 13 Mar 2013.

[25] Mandela, Nelson. "Lighting your Way to a Better Future." At Launch of Mindset Network. *Nelson Mandela Foundation Digital Archive.* 16 July 2003.

[26] Yadav, Dr. Yogendra. "Education Quotations of Mahatma Gandhi." *InternationalPeaceandConflict.org.* 28 Dec. 2012.

[27]Jamrisko, Michelle and Kolet, Ilan. "Cost of College Degree in U.S. Soars 12 Fold: Chart of the Day." *Bloomberg.com.* 15 Aug 2012.

[28] Ellis, Blake. "Average Student Loan Debt: $29,400." *Money.CNN.com.* New York: CNNMoney, 5 Dec 2013.

[29]Bowyer, Chris. "Overqualified and Underemployed: The Job Market Waiting for Graduates." *Forbes/Opinion.* 15 Aug 2014.

[30] Matthews, Chris. "Why College Isn't For Everyone Explained in One Chart." *Fortune.* 5 Sept 2014.

[31] "Programme for International Student Assessment (PISA) 2012/United States." The Organization for Economic Co-operation and Development. *www.oecd.org/PISA.*

[32] Fisman, Ray. "Sweden's School Choice Disaster." *Slate.com.* 15 July 2014.

[33] Shepherd, Jessica. "UK Schools Slip Down World Rankings." *The Guardian.* 7 Dec 2010.

[34] "How Yahoo! Japan Beat eBay at its Own Game." *Business Week.* Bloomberg.com. 3 Jun 2001.

[35] Public domain.

[36] Riley, Geoff. "Revision on Entry Borders." *Business and Economics Blog.* 10 April 2012.

[37] Popkin, Helen A.S. "We Spent 230,060 Years on Social Media in One Month." *CNBC.com.* 4 Dec 2012.

[38] Alter, Diane. "Facebook (NASDAQ FB) Stock Targets at $91 on Whopping Instagram Valuation." *MoneyMorning.com.* 20 Feb 2015.

[39] "Top 10% Authors, as of June 2015." *IDEAS* at the Research Division of the Federal Reserve Bank of St. Louis using RePEc data. https://ideas.repec.org/top/top.person.all.html

[40] "Stats." *Newsroom.fb.com/company-info.*

[41] Maddison, A. *Countours of the World Economy 1-2030 AD.* Oxford: Oxford University Press, 2007.

[42] Markoff, John. "Skilled Work, Without a Worker." *The New York Times.* 18 Aug 2012.

[43] Dunn, Kris. "Probability HR Jobs Will be Lost to Robots in the Next 20 Years?" *HRCapitalist.com.* 24 Jan 2014.

[44] O'Toole, James. "Robots will Replace Fast-Food Workers."

[45] Cook, Dan. "1 in 5 Companies Replace Workers with Machines." *BenefitsPro.com.* 31 Jul 2014.

[46] Scholl, Christopher. "US Army to Replace Human Soldiers with Humanoid Robots." *Global Research News.* 3 Mar 2014.

[47] Kohlsa, Vinod. "Technology will Replace 80% of What Doctors Do." *Fortune.com.* 4 Dec 2012.

[48] "Shutdown." 1 Oct 2013. *Newsday.*

[49] Foster, Peter. "American Shutdown: No Way to Run a Country." Photo gallery "US Government Shutdown: Newspaper Front Pages." *The Telegraph.* 1 Oct 2013.

[50] Kasperkevic, Jana. "Occupy Activists Abolish $3.85m in Corinthian Colleges Students' Loan Debt." *The Guardian.* 17 Sep 2014.

[51] Riva, Adam. "Richest 1% Will Own More than the Rest of the World by 2016." *Dragonfly Effect News.* 28 Jan 2015.

[52] Pandey, Avaneesh. "Global Poverty Levels Halves but More Africans in Extreme Poverty than in 1990: UN Report." *International Business Times.* 8 Jul 2014.

[53] Guildford, Gwynn. "This Might be the Year China's Yawning Trade Surplus Finally Starts Shrinking." *Quartz.* 10 Jan 2014.

[54] Chen, Sharon. "China's Income Equality Surpasses U.S., Posing Risk for Xi." *Bloomberg.com.* 29 Apr 2014.

[55] "Hunger and Policy Fact Sheet." *FeedingAmerica.org.* 2015.

[56] Shah, Anup. "Poverty Around the World." *GlobalIssues.org.* 12 Nov 2011.

[57] The Economist Online. "The 99 Percent." *The Economist.* 26 Oct 2011.

[58] "Inequality: Impacts." "Social Mobility and Education." *The Equality Trust.* London, 2012-2015.

Corak, Miles. "Inequality from Generation to Generation: The United States in Comparison." Ottawa: *University of Ottawa Graduate School of Public and International Affairs,* Jan 2012.

[59] Goldfarb, Zachary A. and Boorstein, Michelle. "Pope Francis Denounces 'Trickle-Down' Economic Theories in Sharp Criticism of Inequality." *The Washington Post.* 26 Nov 2013.

[60] The Shadowed at English Wikipedia. "World War II Casualties." *Wikimedia Commons.* 22 April 2008.svg

[61] Couch, Rich. "Nuclear Warheads: How Low can we Go?" *Let's Talk Books and Politics Blogspot.* 14 Mar 2013.

[62] "Biggest Rises and Falls in the 2014 World Press Freedom Index." *Reporters Without Borders/Reporters sans Frontières.* 31 Jan 2014.

[63] Gongloff, Mark. "China's Economy Just Overtook the U.S. In One Key Measure." *The Huffington Post*. 8 Oct 2014.

[64] Qiao, Niu Yi. "China: Demographic Transition." *Barcelona Field Studies Centre. (GeographyFieldwork.com)*. 27 Feb 2005.

[65] Purdy, Mark. "China's Economy, in Six Charts." *Harvard Business Review*. 29 Nov 2013.

[66] Yuan, Alexander F. "China's Kunming Train Station Violence Leaves 33 Dead." *Radio Free Asia* and *Associated Press*. 2 March 2014.

[67] Editors, Stratfor. "Central Asia and Afghanistan: A Tumultuous History." *Stratfor Global Intelligence*. 24 Sept 2013. With permission of Stratfor.

[68] Kerry, Secretary John. *Remarks after Meeting with Secretary of State of the Holy see Pietro Parolin. 14 Jan 2014.* http://www.state.gov/secretary/remarks/2014/01/219654.htm.

[69] Ogden, Jeff. "Internet users per 100 inhabitants 1997-2014." *Wikimedia Commons*. 5 Apr 2012.

[70] United Stations Department of Economic and Social Affairs. "Report on the World Situation 2010." New York: UN Publications, 2009.

[71] Chen, Shaohua and Ravallion, Martin. *The Developing World is Poorer than We Thought, But No Less Successful in the Fight Against Poverty*. Policy Research Working Paper, The World Bank. Sept 2008.

[72] Dwrcan, Wikimedia Commons User. "Percentage Population Living on Less than $1 per day 2007-2008." UN Human Development Indices 2008. *Commons.Wikimedia.Org*. 21 Apr 2011.

[73] Deaton, Angus. "Income, Health, and Well-Being Around the World: Evidence from the Gallup World Poll." Washington, DC: Gallup, 2008. In "Standard of Living in the Developing World." *Givewell.Org*.

[74] Choi, Amy S. "What the Best Education Systems are Doing Right." *Ideas.Ted.com*. 4 Sept 2014.

[75] Weisenthal, Joe. "Here's the New Ranking of Top Countries in Reading, Science, and Math." *Business Insider*. 3 Dec 2013.

[76] Ripley, Amanda. "The $4 Million Teacher." *Wall Street Journal*.3 Aug 2013.

[77] Hancock, LynNell. "Why Are Finland's Schools Successful?" *Smithsonian Magazine*. Sept 2011.

[78] "Teaching Qualifications in Finland." *www.Helsinki.fi/teachereducation.* 2006.

[79] Lopez, Adam. "How Finnish Schools Shine." *The Guardian.* 9 Apr 2012.

[80] Barret, Victoria. "Bill Gates: It's the Teacher, Stupid." *Forbes.* 26 Jan 2009.

[81] "The American Dream: What is the American Dream?" *Library of Congress Digitized Primary Sources.* Lesson Plan.
www.loc.gov/teachers/classroommaterials/lesson/American-Dream.

Made in the USA
San Bernardino, CA
15 June 2016